LITTLE BOOK OF
GOLF

LITTLE BOOK OF
GOLF

First published in the UK in 2010

© G2 Entertainment Limited 2011

www.G2ent.co.uk

Printed and bound in the EU

ISBN 978-1-907803-38-3

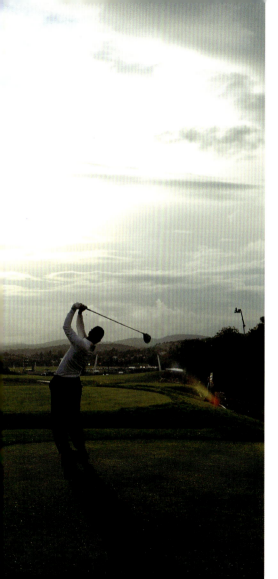

Contents

Ryder Cup 2010

In all of the long and fascinating story of golf, which you can read about from chapter two onwards of this book, few moments have held as much dramatic tension as the few seconds when Hunter Mahan stood hunched over a putt at the 17th green on the final day of the 2010 Ryder Cup.

If this gripping drama had been played out on a West End or Broadway stage, the audience would be preparing to rise to their feet to acclaim the author and cast and the critics would be scurrying away to file their ecstatic reviews.

The players, gathered at the Celtic Manor resort from all corners of Europe and the USA, had played their parts to perfection. The plot, despite being scarcely credible at times, had held spectators spellbound as it followed a tortuous path to its suspense-filled dénouement.

It had all led to this final act, and you could have heard a tee drop on to the south Wales grass as 35,000 spectators clustered around the green. Here's how the plot had left young Mahan needing to sink an 18ft putt to keep alive America's hopes of retaining the venerated trophy:

Act I: After a first session that saw the skies dumping an unwelcome amount of rain on the Usk Valley, America had shaded the opening fourballs 2.5-1.5.

Act II: The following foursomes went America's way too, leaving the defending US team leading 6-4 and Europe looking for inspiration.

Act III: The third session, a mix of foursomes and fourballs, saw a dramatic change in fortunes and was decisively, devastatingly, Europe's. The session tally of 5.5-0.5 left the US staring down the wrong end of a 9.5-6.5 scoreline.

Act IV: But the weather had intervened again, and for the first time in Ryder Cup history, the final session – the singles – was to be played out on a Monday. And it turned out to be a magic Monday, as the headline writers

had been hoping. Digging deep, the Americans battled back in the singles, claiming win after win and finally, incredibly, reaching a match score of 13.5-13.5.

Act V: Enter the last pair, Mahan and Graeme McDowell, doing battle on the par three 17th hole after McDowell had miraculously birdied the 16th to regain a two-hole lead.

This is where we came in. Mahan has fluffed a second-shot chip while McDowell's putt has left him five feet short of the hole. Mahan has to sink his 18-footer if America are not to bid a fond farewell to the trophy.

The putt is on its way and looks to be heading for the hole. At the last second, with European hearts in mouths, it veers away and stays above ground. Mahan accepts the inevitable and offers his hand to McDowell. He has conceded the hole, McDowell is the winner 3&1 and Europe are once again Ryder Cup victors.

Mayhem. Utter mayhem. The roar that erupts from the packed crowd can surely be heard the English side of the Bristol Channel. The European players and non-playing captain Colin Montgomerie are engulfed by enraptured hordes of followers and supporters. The champagne flows and is sprayed by the victorious heroes. Long and loud is the rejoicing.

The defeated but proud Americans face the media and Mahan, poor lad, struggles to hold back the tears while captain Corey Pavin and his team-mates back him to the hilt. His day will come.

The Europeans, too, are overcome by emotion. Montgomerie sums it up when he tells journalists: "I didn't hit a shot, yet it is a proud, proud moment for me personally. It's an amazing feeling to have won." Reflecting for a moment, he realises that it is in fact the proudest moment of his career.

The hero of the hour, Northern Irishman McDowell, is happy to compare this triumph to a rather more personal one – his winning of the US Open three months previously. "The US Open felt like the back nine with my dad back in Portrush compared to this," he insists.

"I was nervous there, boy was I nervous. There was a lot of pressure. The 16th was massive, it was a fast putt and I had to get it going. It's the best putt I've hit in my life.

"I cannot describe the feeling of winning this golf tournament. I was just trying to win it for my team-mates, the caddies and the fans, because everyone's been unbelievable.

"I've never felt as nervous on a golf course in my life as I did out there. I mean, trying to do it for my 11 team-mates, trying to do it for all these people,

◀ Flying the flag: American supporters were optimistic right up until the 17th green of the final pairing

trying to do it for Monty, trying to do it for Europe – it's a lot of pressure."

McDowell's team-mate Lee Westwood had been feeling that pressure too: "I hated every minute of it. I don't know how my wife and parents do it. It's so much easier playing because you're in control. It's always difficult when it's within grabbing distance.

"When you're a player, you understand what Graeme is going through today, and that's what makes it awful because you know how nervous he's going to be, yet you can't do anything about it. You can't say anything to him or do anything."

So the Ryder Cup stays with Europe, at least until the rival teams meet again at the Medinah Country Club, outside Chicago, in the 2012 episode of this most thrilling of sagas. But at Celtic Manor, it looked for long periods as if the US players would be clinging on to the trophy.

The opening day, Friday 1 October, was almost a washout as the rain deluged the valleys, and a mere four hours and a bit of play were possible. The opening fourballs were nicely

◀ Rory McIlroy, who scored two Ryder Cup points and said afterwards: "I would not have said this a year ago, but this is the best event in golf by far."

▶ A happier moment for Hunter Mahan before his 17th green drama

poised as officials glanced nervously at the clouds and prayed for better weather for the days to follow.

Europe claimed the first point when play resumed on the Saturday – Lee Westwood and Martin Kaymer winning 3&2 over Phil Mickelson and Dustin Johnson – but by the time the delayed opening fourballs had finished the Americans had edged in front.

Two of Europe's Irish contingent, McDowell and Rory McIlroy, had fought back from two down to claim a halved match with Matt Kuchar and Stewart Cink, but first Jeff Overton and Bubba Watson recorded a 3&2 victory over Pádraig Harrington and Luke Donald, then Tiger Woods and Steve Stricker did enough for a two-hole win over Ross Fisher and Ian Poulter.

The session ended with McDowell paying handsome tribute to his playing partner, who was about to go on and make an indelible mark on the event. "This kid was unbelievable this morning," said the man we had all come to call G-Mac. "We struggled yesterday but this guy was off the charts this morning. He's one of the best players in the world and one of the best

I've ever seen."

Super Sunday dawned … eventually. The rain made an unwelcome return – making some parts of the course resemble a paddling pool and others an African waterhole trampled by hippos – and play did not get under way until 1.30pm. But by the end of play, Europe were more than satisfied with their day's work.

Starting the afternoon ahead in all six matches on the course, the Europeans quite simply obliterated their opponents, taking the session five and a half points to a half and leaving themselves in what looked like a comfortable lead. They had been trailing by 6-4. Now they were ahead 9.5-6.5.

First, in the foursomes, Westwood and Donald saw off the challenge of Woods and Stricker in magnificent style and short order, 6&5. Then McDowell and McIlroy further enhanced their reputations with a 3&1 win over Mahan and Zach Johnson.

In the fourballs, the good news kept coming for Europe. Harrington and Fisher kept up the winning momentum with a 2&1 win against Jim Furyk and

Rickie Fowler, then Peter Hanson and Miguel Angel Jiménez (the latter starring at the ripe old age of 46) beat off Watson and Overton 2-up. Poulter and Kaymer chalked up a 2&1 win over Mickelson and Fowler, and then it was the turn of a pair of Italian brothers to take centre stage.

Senior brother Edoardo and Francesco Molinari, hailing from Turin, shared a point with Cink and Kuchar, but only after Francesco had won the hearts of Europe supporters with a sublime piece of golf. The brothers were one down at the 18th, but Francesco plonked his third shot a few feet from the pin and holed out for the birdie that was necessary to share the honours.

So the match, in unprecedented fashion, was heading for a fourth day and Europe were sitting pretty. They needed to take a mere five points from the 12 singles matches to ensure victory, while the Americans needed to score an unlikely eight. And would you believe it, they almost did it, after a day during which the match seesawed violently. The US team spat on its hands and set off on its own 12-step

programme to recovery.

Step 1: Johnson, peering through the morning mist, polished off Kaymer to the tune of 6&4. The American fightback had begun.

Step 2: Stricker shrugged off the disappointment of his thrashing in the foursomes by dispensing with Westwood, ranked number two in the world, 2&1. Another point to the US.

Step 3: A step backwards for America as Ian Poulter made short work of Kuchar 5&4 and Europe edged nearer the finishing line.

Step 4: McIlroy, at the tender age of 21, produced the goods once more to halve his match with Cink and take the match score to 11-9.

Step 5: After apparently coasting at three up with five to play, Donald staggered home on the 18th green against Furyk. It was now 12-9; surely the match was in Europe's pocket?

Step 6: More good news for Europe – Jiménez wrapped up a 4&3 win over the left-handed Watson. One and a half points to go and Europe would be home and dry.

Step 7: Overton was not beaten yet, and he pressed home the point by

The proudest moment: captain Colin Montgomerie with his victorious Europe team handing a 3&2 defeat to Fisher. Score: 13-10.

Step 8: If spectators thought they had seen the best or last of Tiger in the match, they were badly mistaken.

Woods showed his true mettle by blasting through his last seven holes in seven under par, demolishing Francesco Molinari and winning 4&3. Were we about to witness the comeback to end

LITTLE BOOK OF **GOLF**

them all? Score: 13-11.

Step 9: You thought it couldn't continue? Wrong. The wily, experienced Mickelson had drawn a complete blank in his previous matches, but now he drew on everything he had ever learned about golf to swat Hanson aside 4&2. Score: 13-12.

Step 10: It was down to Harrington to steady the wallowing European ship and beat Johnson, but the Iowan was having none of it. He prevailed 3&2 and the match score was now tied at 13 apiece.

Step 11: The US rookie Fowler stretched European nerves to breaking point as, playing Edoardo Molinari, he came back from the dead – three down with three to play – with a trio of birdies to claim a halved match that had not seemed possible. Score: 13.5-13.5.

Step 12: Cometh the hour, cometh the man. And the man was Graham McDowell. He needed to win that 17th hole. Hunter Mahan also needed to win the hole. The Irishman held his nerve while the man from Orange, California lost his. McDowell won 3&1 and the final match score was 14.5-13.5.

It was, as they say, all over bar the shouting, although there was a lot of that going on in the streets, living rooms, pubs and cafes of Europe that night. For the sixth time in the last eight Ryder Cups, the European team had emerged victorious.

Many players on both sides contributed enormously to the incredible spectacle that was the 2010 Ryder Cup, but special mention must go to the wise and doughty European captain.

As a player Colin Montgomerie saw it all, playing in eight Ryder Cups from 1991 to 2006 and being unbeaten in 20 of his 36 matches. He knew what was needed to win the thing, and he made sure his players knew too, motivating, cajoling, urging, encouraging, supporting, consoling and applauding at exactly the right moments. There were times when he couldn't bear to watch the play; there were moments when he seemed to be playing himself.

Afterwards, as he stood down from the Ryder Cup captaincy and recommended Jose Maria Olazabal for the 2012 job, he realised that nothing in the world of golf could top what he was feeling at that moment. European supporters knew exactly how he felt.

◀ European hands on the trophy: from left, Lee Westwood, Ian Poulter, Luke Donald and Ross Fisher

Origins
of Golf

Where it began, no one knows. The origin is lost in the mists of time.

It might have been on a road in Normandy, or in a Roman alley. It might have been in dunes above the North Sea or on a hill overlooking Peking. It might have been in a Flemish field or a London courtyard, or on a frozen Dutch canal.

No one can say where or when golf was born, but one thing is certain: no other recreation has so transfixed its practitioners.

Hardly a country remains untouched by the golf epidemic. Its lure is hard to define, impossible to exaggerate. It's an obsession that can begin at any age and last a lifetime.

Golf's appeal stems from one of man's primal urges: to strike an object with a stick. Envisage homo erectus swatting stones or bones with a tree limb. So golf is older than civilisation itself.

Depending on whom we believe, the first golf shots were struck between 2,000 and 600 years ago. The Roman Empire's soldiers played paganica, hitting a feather-stuffed ball with curved sticks. But evidence suggests this was a team sport, and the ball was moving.

Scrolls from the Ming Dynasty (mid- to late-1300s) depict suigan – "a game in which you hit a ball with a stick while walking". Silk traders might have exported this game to Europe.

A 14th century stained-glass window in Gloucester Cathedral shows a figure wielding a stick with a golf-like backswing. But this might have been a game called cambuca.

Across the Channel, the French had a game called jeu de mail: a blend of billiards, croquet and miniature golf played with mallets and wooden balls. It caught on in England, where it became the rage of the ruling class under the name 'pall mall', after the famous London street. Charles I was an avid player.

By the 18th century, this game had played out, except in southern France, where Basques would hit over hill and dale to targets such as barns.

In Belgium, chole was played, using iron clubs and an egg-shaped wooden ball. Two teams bid on the number of shots needed to hit a distant target. The low-bidding team took three strokes; their opponents had one stroke to send the ball into trouble. The offence took three more strokes, followed by one for

▲ The ancient game of pall mall being played in a more modern era

of the Scottish game comes from the Dutch, who in the 13th century played a game with more than a passing similarity to golf. Its name? Colf.

In 1296 the Dutch had a colf course, stretching 4,500 yards for just four holes – or doors, rather – to a kitchen, a windmill, a castle, and a courthouse. Balls were pursued through churchyards and town centres and ultimately, the colfers were banished to the countryside. In winter, they shot towards poles on frozen lakes and rivers.

Colf was popular in Holland for at least 400 years. By the early 1700s, however, it had vanished, in all probability to Scotland. Note the connection between 'colf' and 'golf'; the implements and balls used were similar; and there is geographic evidence.

By 1650, golf was well rooted in a dozen towns on Scotland's east coast, a short sail from Holland. Scots exported wooden clubs to the Dutch, who returned the compliment with rudimentary colf balls. And paintings show Scots playing a stick-and-ball game on ice.

It was the Scots who gave golf its unique character; who combined

the defence, and so on until the bid was hit or missed.

Whether these games of the Renaissance era bore any resemblance to golf is of little consequence, because by that time golf was well entrenched along Scotland's east coast.

The best argument for a forefather

distance off the tee with deftness around the green; who ingrained the notion of players advancing independently towards a hole.

The first written evidence of golf is a parliamentary decree banning it, for reasons of national security. In 1457, James II of Scotland declared "that futeball and golfe be utterly cryit doune and nocht usit". It seems the Scots, at war with England, had been neglecting archery practice in favour of golf.

When James IV married the daughter of England's Henry IV, the conflict with the English ended – and so did the conflict with golfers. James IV became the first of a long line of golfing royals, and legend has it that

▼ Golf in 1862: a couple of golfers watched by their caddies. Note the tees, made from mounds of earth

ORIGINS OF GOLF

▶ Golf circa 1790: an elegant gentleman is accompanied by his caddy

▼ Seventeenth century golf: note the primitive club and large, feather-stuffed ball

Mary Queen of Scots teed it up the day after her husband, Lord Darnley, was murdered in 1567.

In 1604, the King of England appointed a royal clubmaker, and soon after, a seven-hole course was laid out near London, on the Black Heath. Royal Blackheath still sits there today.

Despite royal approval, golf was open to anyone with a couple of clubs and a ball. It was an informal activity, with no rules, few guidelines and no formal competitions.

Golfers learned to hit the ball on a low trajectory, keeping it under the sea breezes: feet far apart, bodies aimed to the right of the target, ball positioned well back in the stance and knees deeply bent. The club was whipped around the body horizontally and the ball flew a few feet above the ground. It would then run on after hitting the hard turf of the links.

As the game spread, methods developed, word of great play travelled and a desire arose to find the best golfer in the land. In 1744, golfers from the Links at Leith persuaded the city of Edinburgh to provide a silver club as the prize for an annual competition. The event was open to "Noblemen or Gentlemen or other Golfers, from any part of Great Britain or Ireland" and the winner would be called 'The Captain of the Golf'.

Ten local men played and the prize went to John Rattray with a score of 60 for two trips around the five-hole course – holes ranged from 414 to 495 yards. The event is recognised as golf's first organised competition, and the Leith golfers are credited with forming the first bona fide club: the Honourable Company of Edinburgh Golfers.

But that day something even more important happened: golf was played according to a set of rules.

They were brief – just 13 in all – and charitable, with no penalties for violations. The first rule stated: "You must tee your ball within a club-length of the hole." Imagine how craggy those early putting greens must have been.

Indeed, golf's first fields bore little resemblance to today's manicured meadows. The Scottish courses were set on linksland: barren, undulating terrain that separated beaches from arable ground. The sandy subsoil drained well but supported only long grasses and thick brush, making it of little value except to rabbits and sheep.

These herbivores served as golf's first greenkeepers – and played a role in course design by burrowing into the turf as protection against the elements. As the wind enlarged the burrows, bunkers took shape.

Those original courses had no tees, fairways or greens, just a hole in the ground every few hundred yards, but one might be as shallow as a rabbit scrape, the next so deep that retrieving the ball was a major achievement.

There was no set number of holes, either, with courses running according to the lay of the land. While the Links at Leith had five holes, nearby North Berwick sported seven. There was a 12-holer at Prestwick, and Montrose

▼ The first Open Golf Championship, 1860: golfers gather outside the St Andrews clubhouse

ORIGINS OF GOLF

▶ Golf in the 18ᵗʰ century: measuring up a shot at Edinburgh

▼ Golf circa1910: in Mann's bunker on the links at the Royal Portman Golf Club

weighed in with a whopping 25. In time, a standard would be set, and the authority for that decree would come from the bastion of golf administration: the little town of St Andrews on Scotland's east coast.

For golfers, St Andrews means one thing: the grandest of all links, the Old Course. Written evidence of golf at St Andrews dates from 1552, but most historians agree the game was played there in one form or another for at least 300 years before that.

St Andrews' golfers did not organise themselves into a club until 1754. On May 14, "twenty-two Noblemen and Gentlemen being admirers of the ancient and healthful exercise of the Golf" formed The Society of St Andrews Golfers and adopted the 13 rules set down by the Edinburgh golfers.

The first step towards St Andrews

becoming the world's golf capital came in 1764, when the St Andreans made a revision to their playground. At that time, the Old Course consisted of 12 holes. Golfers played 11 holes out to the far end, turned and threaded their way home, playing 10 of the holes backwards to the same cups before finishing at a solitary hole near the start. Thus, a round consisted of 22 holes.

But in 1764, the Society decided to convert the first four holes into two. Since this change shortened the same four holes to two on the road in, the round was reduced from 22 holes to 18, which would become the world standard.

Over the following years, the Society attracted the best and brightest golfers, framed new rules and positioned itself as the last word on all matters golf. When, in 1834, King William IV became the Society's patron and declared it the Royal & Ancient Golf Club, the pre-eminence of St Andrews was assured.

In 1834, however, there wasn't much golf to oversee. Only 17 clubs existed: 14 of them in Scotland, two in England and one in India. Throughout the world, fewer than a thousand people could call themselves golfers. And more than a few were women.

In 1811, Musselburgh fishwives participated in the first known women's tournament. The first women's club, St Andrews Ladies' Golf Club, was formed in 1867 and the Ladies' Golf Union followed in 1893, with the first official Ladies' Championship not far behind.

The first three championships were won by Lady Margaret Scott, who was known for a long backswing, tremendous distance and scores in the 80s. After her third championship, Lady Margaret retired undefeated.

Doing less well, however, was the game itself. In the early 1800s, golf was shrinking. What a century earlier had been a recreation of the masses had eroded into a diversion for the wealthy and privileged.

Why? Above all, because of the ball.

▼ What the ladies were wearing circa 1890: golfer Isette Pearson

Development of the Game

▼ Two early featheries, circa 1850

The first golf balls, believed to have been made of boxwood, lacked sophistication but were at least affordable. But in the early 17th century a new ball, the feathery, was put in play.

Consisting of a leather cover stuffed with goose or chicken breast feathers, it was about 1.6in in diameter but weighed only three-quarters of an ounce, about half that of a modern ball. The feathery provided resilience and distance: the strongest players could hit it over 200 yards.

A strip of bull or horse hide was soaked in alum water, then cut into two circles and a strip for the middle. These were sewn together, soaked again and turned inside out. Into a small hole the ballmaker stuffed the feathers (which had been boiled to make them malleable) with a 'brogue': a blunt-edged iron spike topped with a wooden crosspiece on which he leaned. When he had crammed in about a top hat-full of feathers, he sewed up the hole.

As the ball dried, the feathers expanded while the cover contracted, producing a hard sphere. The feathery was then hammered as round as possible and painted for protection against the elements.

Even the best craftsmen could produce no more than four balls a day, and featheries were 12 times more costly than wooden balls. What's more, one off-centre slash with an iron could knock the stuffing out of it, and players invariably required three or four balls per round.

▲ Gutta Percha balls, circa 1890

◄ The Haskell ball transformed the game at the beginning of the 20th century

▼ A world away from the feathery: the modern golf ball makes the game more straightforward

What was needed was an inexpensive, weatherproof and more rounded ball; one whose performance, durability and affordability would attract more people to golf. In the mid-19th century, that ball arrived in the form of gutta percha, the coagulated milk of a Malayan gum tree.

The substance was exported in sheets, which the ballmaker cut into strips, softened in hot water and rounded by hand. The ball was then dropped in cold water to harden. If a 'gutty' became bruised or cracked, it could be resoftened and made whole again.

The first gutties were rounder than feather balls but, with no markings on their surface, they were tough to get airborne and tended to duck or dive in flight.

Willie Dunn, a Musselburgh professional, noticed his caddies were hitting gutties with more authority than he could muster from a feathery. The reason? Nicks and scuffs: once it had a few cuts, the gutty flew like a champion. So entered the hand-hammered gutty, with

DEVELOPMENT OF THE GAME

pre-chiselled aerodynamic markings.

Craftsmen began cranking out a hundred gutties a day, and tradesmen, artisans and peasants once again thronged the links. By 1890, the smattering of golf clubs in Great Britain had grown to 387 and golf had reached every outpost of the British Empire.

But the arrival of the gutty was met with opposition by one faction: the feathery makers, chief among whom was Allan Robertson of St Andrews.

Allan was the finest golfer of his time, is credited with being the game's first professional and was probably its first course architect and green superintendent.

But the gutty threatened Robertson's livelihood. He made his employees promise never to use the ball, which led to a rift between him and his chief apprentice Tom Morris, who agreed to shun the gutty but was caught out. He claimed he'd run out of featheries and was forced to borrow a ball, but Robertson was unconvinced. Morris opened his own gutty shop, first in St Andrews and later in Prestwick.

In time, Robertson gave in to the gutty, and he was also among the first to realise that the new ball required new clubs.

Golf had been played with essentially the same assortment of mallets for more than two centuries. The woods had shafts of hazelwood or ash with heads of apple or thornwood. The two pieces of wood were spliced together, glued and bound with tarred twine. The grips were of soft sheepskin.

The play club was a long-nosed weapon with little loft in its tiny, high hitting area. Its shaft was 45in long but it met the clubhead at an angle of 120 degrees, forcing golfers to stand well away from the ball and contributing to

the flat, around-the-body swing.

Lofted woods called spoons – because their faces were curved like the bowl of

▲ Manufacture of Silver King golf balls in 1932

a spoon – were used for approach play, from the long spoon for distance shots to the baffing spoon for raising the ball from poor lies and over hazards.

A golfer might carry as many as three putters, also made of wood: in addition to the traditional putter there was the driving putter for hitting low tee shots into the wind and the approach putter for bumping the ball in to the green. All were lofted.

Iron clubs were for dire circumstances, as suggested by their names: bunker iron, rut iron and track iron. Their heads had concave faces and snubbed-off toes.

As the ball changed, so did the clubs. The hard gutty yielded little at impact and wood clubs tended to crack on contact. So clubs appeared with shafts of a softer wood – hickory – and with less torsion: the clubhead lagged less far behind the hands during the downswing, which would lead eventually to a more up-and-down swing.

The clubheads also changed, to softer beechwood that absorbed the hit better, and became shorter and thicker to pack more punch. The ultimate effect of all of this was to lessen the strain on the

spliced area just above the clubhead.

Iron clubs became the preferred implements for approach shots, and several Scottish blacksmiths took up clubmaking full-time, under the title 'cleekmaker'. The cleek – equivalent to the modern 2- or 3-iron – was followed by the more lofted mid-iron, mashie and niblick.

Allan Robertson embraced the new irons as a craftsman and a player, and was probably the first to master

▼ Opening of the golf season at St Andrews, 1876

DEVELOPMENT OF THE GAME

the run-up shot with a cleek. At St Andrews in 1858, he ran his approach on to the 18th green then rolled in for a total of 79, making him the first to break 80 on the Old Course.

A year later, Robertson fell sick with hepatitis and died aged 44. His death left a void in professional golf, and there was an urge to fill it. Tom Morris and Musselburgh's Willie Park were Scotland's leading players and rail travel had brought them within easy reach of courses.

In 1860, the Prestwick Club announced a championship for professionals, with a red Moroccan leather belt embroidered with silver medallions as the prize. Only eight men entered the first event, and the winner was Willie Park with an unimpressive 174 for 36 holes. The scores were so high that a number of amateurs felt they might do better, so the next year the competition was opened to all. And the Open Championship has remained so ever since.

When Tom Morris won the Championship for the last time, in 1868 at the age of 46, he became, and remains, the oldest Open Champion. One year later, the title was won by a lad of 17 years – still the youngest champion. His name was also Tom Morris and this father-son duo would forever be known as Old and Young Tom.

Young Tom defended his title successfully in 1869 and took permanent possession of the belt with a third straight win in 1870.

There was a gap in Open play in 1871 for lack of a prize. Then, in 1872, St Andrews, Musselburgh and Prestwick presented a silver claret jug, and the three sites began a club-to-club rotation principle that continues today.

'Tommy' picked up where he'd left off, winning the title at Prestwick for a fourth time. He might have won it many more times had he not died aged 24.

In September 1875, as the Morris father-son team were closing out a match at North Berwick, Old Tom received a telegram, and told his son they had to leave immediately: Young Tom's wife and newborn had died in childbirth. The young man played golf only twice more before passing away. The clinical cause of death was likely pneumonia but, in the lore of golf, Young Tom Morris died of a broken heart.

Old Tom outlived his son by 33 years, returning to the Royal & Ancient Golf Club as its first resident

professional. With his long grey beard, tweed cap and pipe, Tom Morris was a familiar figure to all who passed by his shop near the 18th green.

▲ 'Young' Tom Morris wearing the British Open belt, which he won four times

Spreading the
Gospel of Golf

Golf took its time to reach the masses, but when it did, it spread like wildfire. The period from the mid-19th century to the beginning of the 1900s witnessed an explosion in participation.

Around 1860 there were 30 golf clubs in Scotland and three in England. By 1900 there were more than 2,000 clubs across the whole of Britain. Two main forces drove the boom.

First, the gutty, about a quarter of the price of the feathery, brought the game within reach of a wider audience. And enough gutties could be made to meet increased demand for balls.

Expansion of the railways was the other influence. More people started to take holidays, and seaside resorts built golf courses to attract visitors.

The Open Championship went from strength to strength. From 1872,

a steadily increasing number of entrants competed for the Claret Jug and, with Old Tom Morris past his best, it was left to a new guard to take over. Jamie Anderson, a St Andrews man, seized the opportunity, winning the championship three times in a row from 1877–79, and Bob Ferguson followed with a hat-trick of victories from 1880–82.

The performances of two great amateurs lit up the Open in the final decade of the 19th century. John Ball became the first golfer from outside Scotland to win, in 1890, and in his footsteps followed Harold Hilton, like Ball from the Royal Liverpool Golf Club.

Hilton's first Open victory at Muirfield in 1892, the first 72-hole championship, was sealed with a total

America and, in Morris' shop, purchased six clubs and two dozen gutties. Six months later, Lockhart's friend and fellow Scot John Reid assembled with five other gentlemen in a cow pasture in New York, to give golf a try.

◀ The home of golf: St Andrews in 1905

▼ Harold Hilton, Open champion in 1892 and 1897; four-time Amateur Champion and US Amateur Champion in 1911

of 305 – which was not bettered for more than a decade – and he won again in 1897. And in 1911 he became the only Brit ever to win the US Amateur Championship.

Golf in Britain was soaring, yet in America it had barely taken off. Old Tom Morris played a role in changing that.

Scottish linen merchant Robert Lockhart visited his shop at St Andrews in 1887. Lockhart, who had emigrated to the US but whose job frequently took him to Scotland, decided to introduce the game to friends in

SPREADING THE GOSPEL

▼ Three-time Open champion Jamie Anderson inspects clubs at St Andrews

All six became instant converts and founded a club they named the St Andrew's Golf Club, in honour of the home of golf. So 14 November 1888 became the official beginning of golf in the United States.

Within five years of the founding of St Andrew's, dozens of clubs had opened, aided by a stream of emigrant Scottish professionals. Scots had also spread the gospel of golf to all corners of the British Empire.

India was the first to receive the game, with the opening of the Royal Calcutta Golf Club. Australia followed with Royal Melbourne in 1891 and New Zealand, Mauritius, Canada, Hong Kong and South Africa were next. In continental Europe, too, golf was getting a grip: France and Belgium were among the first to build courses.

While many Scottish professionals were in a hurry to get to the US, Charles Blair Macdonald went the other way. The son of a wealthy Chicagoan, Macdonald sailed to St Andrews in 1872 at the age of 16 to study. His grandfather bought him a set of clubs at Old Tom Morris' shop, and soon he was spending every spare moment on the Old Course, learning from the great players.

Two years later, Macdonald returned to the States with a passion for the game. But, since the US was devoid of courses, he made do for 15 years playing on trips to Britain.

Once America got the golf bug, however, Macdonald was ready. In 1894, a group of amateurs assembled at the Newport Golf Club in Rhode Island to determine a national champion, and CB was the man to beat.

But when he lost by a stroke to William Lawrence, Macdonald protested that a stone wall, which had cost him two strokes, was not a legitimate hazard, and that a proper championship should be decided in a head-to-head format.

He got his wish when St Andrew's held a second amateur championship, this one at matchplay. Macdonald defeated Lawrence in the semi-finals, but, after halving the final match, lost to Lawrence Stoddard in a play-off. This time he argued the result was invalid because one club may not presume to run a national championship.

Lawrence Curtis, of the Country Club in Brookline, Massachusetts, and St Andrew's founder Henry Tallmadge agreed to invite representatives of clubs to form a body to conduct national championships and further the interests of the game. And so, in

December 1894, the United States Golf Association was founded.

The association's first president was businessman Theodore Havemeyer, with Macdonald settling for second vice-president. A year later, however, Macdonald got what he really wanted – a victory in the USGA's first Amateur Championship, held at Newport. Macdonald blazed to a 12&11 victory over Charles Sands, a young tennis buff who had played golf for just three months.

The next day, 21-year-old Englishman Horace Rawlins bettered nine fellow professionals and one amateur to become the first United

▲ Golfer's delight: the sixth hole at Muirfield, home of the Honourable Company of Edinburgh Golfers

SPREADING THE GOSPEL

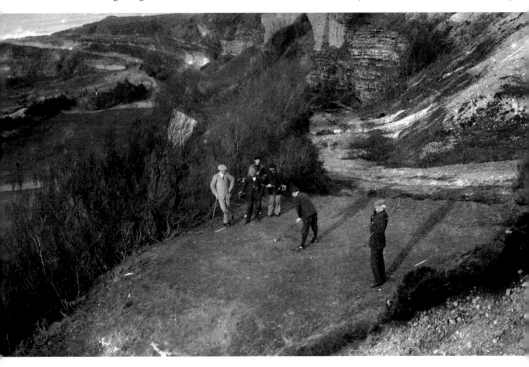

▼ Golf spreads to France: the links at Biarritz, circa 1910

States Open Champion.

Macdonald's breakthrough was also his swansong – he never won another championship – but he did have a lasting influence on the game, as America's first great golf course architect.

In 1895 his bold design at the Chicago Golf Club – a seaside-type course set a thousand miles from the sea – became America's first 18-hole course. But Macdonald's masterpiece was a layout on the eastern end of Long

Island, a course he modestly named The National Golf Links of America.

Macdonald poured several years and many thousands of his dollars into it, and when the National opened in 1911, it set a new standard for American golf architecture. In the clubhouse is a life-sized bronze statue of CB Macdonald. Legend claims he commissioned it himself and billed members for it.

CB wasn't afraid to feed his ego in his course design. He routed the Chicago Golf Club's holes in a clockwise circle to favour the left-to-right drift of his shots. Spray the ball to the right and your worst penalty was light rough; spray it left and you were in a cornfield. Since this inequity was too severe, a three-word phrase – out of bounds – made its debut in the rule book of 1899.

Americans wanted to play with the graceful pivot, dazzling footwork and overlapping grip that Harry Vardon had made famous.

However, while the great man's technique was much admired, the golf ball that bore his name, the Vardon Flyer, had just about flown its last. Another new ball made its way to the

▲ Golf in Canada: an old Douglas fir on the 15th at Banff Springs, Alberta, circa 1939

tee. And it changed everything.

Coburn Haskell was an entrepreneur and keen golfer who dreamed of longer drives. One day, visiting the offices of the BF Goodrich rubber company, Haskell noticed a basket full of elastic thread.

He had a brainstorm – he could wind those thin strands of rubber around an inner core and make a golf ball that would surely be more resilient and lively than a gutty. Haskell got a ball wadded up and persuaded BF Goodrich to fashion a gutta percha cover for it.

The result was America's first major golf invention: the Haskell ball. It flew fully 20 yards farther than the gutty and hit the ground running. Initially, increased bounce and roll made the Haskell difficult to control, but for anyone in need of distance, it made golf a different game.

After short-hitting Walter Travis used it to win the 1901 US Amateur, the ball known as 'Bounding Billy' was embraced by America and soon the Goodrich Company was mass-producing them on an automatic winding machine.

It had its critics, among them the Briton Sandy Herd who, on the eve of the 1902 Open championship, denounced the ball as unfit. But during a practice round, Herd got a lesson in playing the Haskell from amateur John Ball, and changed his mind. The 1902 Open went to Herd by one stroke over Vardon, still flogging the ill-fated Flyer.

The Haskell changed everything, beginning with the implements that struck the new ball. The softer, more springy Haskell required woods with a harder hit, and persimmon became the tree of choice, with inserts of various materials. Iron heads were enlarged and scored with grooves to help impart backspin, and clubs with extra loft were added; the key was now not simply to make the ball go but also to make it stop.

The ball also turned out to be salvo number one in an endless battle between technology and golf course design.

Hitherto, American golf architecture had been a matter of quantity rather than quality. Equipment maker AG Spalding had dispatched a certain Tom Bendelow across America to serve as architect for anyone who wanted a course. Bendelow had no particular knowledge or training, but he had a Scottish accent and he worked for just $25 per design. He also worked quickly, perpetrating more than 600 courses, most of them mediocre.

But the new and better ball commanded new and better courses, so architects went back to their drawing boards, designing longer layouts and adding thou-

▼ 'The penal school of golf course architecture': the third hole at Oakmont, Pennsylvania

SPREADING THE GOSPEL

▼ 'A relentless examination in shot making and strategy': the ninth hole of the Pine Valley Golf Course

sands of yards to those that existed.

In Pittsburgh, Henry and William Fownes unveiled Oakmont, with long, narrow fairways, more than 200 bunkers and 18 fiercely sloped greens that were maintained at breakneck speed. With Oakmont, the penal school of golf course architecture was born.

Golf's first top-notch resort course began to take shape when in 1901 Donald Ross emigrated from Royal Dornoch in Scotland to the sandhills of North Carolina and started work on Pinehurst Number 2. At the same time, hotel owner George Crump became obsessed with constructing the world's hardest golf course.

With the aid of English architect Harry Colt, he created Pine Valley in New Jersey. With every fairway and green set off by sand and scrub, it was a relentless examination in shot making and strategy. When Pine Valley opened in 1913, other designers hailed it as America's finest course, and in many observers' eyes it still is.

Three more Philadelphians would leave indelible marks on golf course design: Albert Tillinghast (mostly in the East, with Winged Foot and Baltusrol his monuments); George Thomas (a pair of gems at Riviera and the Los Angeles Country Club in Southern California); and Hugh Wilson (a masterpiece at Merion).

New courses were more playable and enjoyable than their predecessors, because of the advent in 1913 of the power mower. Fairways and greens could now be maintained swiftly and meticulously, and golf would never be the same again.

▲ A masterpiece designed by Hugh Wilson: the 418 yard, par four fifth hole, with the par three third green behind, on the East Course at Merion, Pennsylvania

The Great Triumvirate

Harry Vardon

To many golfers, the name Vardon describes the grip they use, the little finger of the right hand riding piggyback on the forefinger of the left hand. To followers of American professional golf, it's the name on the trophy for the tour's leading player in the stroke averages.

If you place 'Harry' in front of the surname, however, you have one of the most influential characters who ever played the game. Harry Vardon was a golfing pioneer, and his influence was almost revolutionary.

Born in Jersey in 1870, Vardon started caddying at a young age and was smitten by the game. His elder brother turned professional first, but Harry soon followed in his footsteps and quickly established himself as the superior golfer.

By his early 20s, this elegant swinger was playing like no other golfer. He could fade it, draw it, knock it down or loft it up, but most of all he could hit it straight – very straight.

Vardon's game was all about precision. He was a slimly built fellow without the physical presence to overpower a golf course, but he knew how to break down its defences with guile and skill. Driving the ball as straight as he did meant he was more often than not playing shots from the fairway, and he capitalised by becoming a great iron player.

He was a fine putter until his late 30s, by which time he was suffering from the 'yips'. Not that he let it stop him winning tournaments: Vardon's grit easily matched his physical skills.

He won the 1914 Open Championship at the age of 44 years and 42 days, the oldest man to do so since Old Tom Morris in 1867.

◀ 'One of the most influential characters who ever played the game': Harry Vardon

THE GREAT TRIUMVIRATE

come over the next 14 years. But this was his opportunity to make his mark in front of a new audience, and he seized it.

Vardon won with a display of patient, precision golf that lent something of an inevitable air to his game – a characteristic that opponents could find dispiriting.

Vardon wasn't one for animated gestures or shouting about his talents, but his gifts were there for all to see in his shots and, in his prime, he was unshakeable mentally. He was, without a shadow of a doubt, the world's best golfer at that time.

He went on to play in two more US Opens, and he finished second on both occasions. The second of those runner-up spots was when he was 50, not in good health but still talented enough to hold a four-shot lead with seven holes to play.

In his heyday, it would have been unthinkable for Vardon to let the title slip through his fingers, but he was weakened by illness and that ultimately proved his undoing. His major winning days were over, but what a time he'd had of it.

Roberto de Vicenzo, victor in 1967, is the only man to win an Open in its present format at an older age than Vardon – and then by only 51 days.

The 1900 US Open in Chicago was a defining moment for Vardon. He already had three Open Championships to his credit and three more would

▲ Two of the
Triumvirate
square up:
James Braid
plays Harry
Vardon at
Sandy Lodge,
Northwood

James Braid

During Vardon's playing career, only two players in Britain could give him more than a decent game: sturdy fellow Englishman JH Taylor and bushy-moustached Scot James Braid. For the best part of 20 years, the trio dominated the game and became known as 'The Great Triumvirate'.

Braid, a popular, colourful character, was tall and powerful, an awesome hitter, with big hands and an aggressive swing. He wasn't the straightest of hitters but that wasn't a problem, because Braid had a very fine touch around the greens.

Born just down the road from St Andrews, Braid was from a poor family and golf did not find him easily. However, he soon developed into a fine player, although he was the last of the Great Triumvirate to hit the big time.

But Braid was soon winning major trophies like a man in a hurry. Before he had won his first Open, Harry Vardon had three to his name, yet Braid was the first man to win five Opens, in an extraordinary 10-year spell.

Braid was exciting to watch, with the same attacking style employed later by Arnold Palmer and Seve Ballesteros. Galleries relished the fact that one never knew what was coming next, but it was invariably worth watching.

Braid became the first club professional at Walton Heath in Surrey and was also a prolific designer, responsible for dozens of courses all over Britain. His legacy lives on in such classic layouts as the King's Course at Gleneagles, St Enodoc in Cornwall and Blairgowrie Rosemount in Scotland.

James Braid: five-time Open Championship winner

JH Taylor

▼ Designed
by Braid: the
sixth hole at
St Enodoc,
Cornwall

Before Braid came on the scene, JH Taylor was Vardon's greatest rival. Indeed, he was something of a young prodigy, winning a couple of Open Championships before Vardon had opened his account.

Taylor, who grew up playing on the links of Westward Ho! In Devon, had a tidy, compact swing and his speciality was low, punchy iron shots. He was sturdy, with a low centre of gravity and excellent balance, and had the qualities to play great golf in windy conditions.

Taylor thrived on the Open's windswept links courses, and he had the ideal temperament to go with his all-round game. Remaining calm at all times gave him the ability to choose the right shots under pressure, and he knew

how to grasp a winning opportunity.

It was no surprise when Taylor fired a record first-round 75 in the 1893 Open at Prestwick. He failed to win that year, but that supreme round was a taste of things to come.

At the next Open, at Sandwich, he became the first Englishman to win the

▲ Thriving on the links: JH Taylor plays a shot during the Open at St Andrews

THE GREAT TRIUMVIRATE

▶ The Great
Triumvirate and a
US Open winner:
from left, JH
Taylor, James
Braid, Harry
Vardon and Fred
Herd

Championship, on the first occasion the event was held outside Scotland.

When the Championship returned to St Andrews the following year, Taylor won it again. Twelve months later at Muirfield, he was within a whisker of a hat-trick but, having tied with Vardon after 72 holes, he lost the two-round playoff. Nevertheless, it was the start of an impressive Open sequence for Taylor.

Perhaps his finest achievement was at the 1900 Open at St Andrews, where he produced the lowest score in every round and left Braid and Vardon trailing. That same year he came close in the US Open, but was pipped by Vardon.

Taylor designed many fine courses, including his beloved Royal Mid–Surrey, where he became the pro, and Datchet, near Windsor. He also helped elevate the status of his fellow professionals.

He was a speaker of high regard, articulate and much in demand for public engagements. And he is regarded as the man most responsible for setting up the fledgling Professional Golfers' Association.

The Ultimate
Amateur

Bobby Jones

He was only 14 when he burst on the scene in the 1916 US Amateur at Merion, but Robert Tyre Jones Jnr was already well known in his native Georgia. A year earlier he had shot a course-record 68 at the East Lake Country Club in Atlanta, where he had been club champion at the age of 12. And two weeks before heading north, he had beaten men twice his age to become Georgia State Amateur Champion.

At Merion, Jones made his way through two matches before losing to defending champion Bob Gardner, while captivating everyone with his long drives, crisp irons and fearless assault on the course.

In those days, Jones' only weakness was his temper. Prone to fits of extreme anger, he cursed like a docker and threw clubs at the smallest provocation. In time, he learned to control his fire, and there then flourished a grand career.

From 1923 to 1930, Jones won four US Opens, three British Opens, five US Amateurs and one British Amateur – a total of 13 national championships. Of his last 12 Opens – nine US, three British – he won seven, and in four of the other five he was runner-up.

No other player has come close to matching this phenomenal record – and Jones compiled it while playing no more often than the average duffer.

An amateur to the core, he put his family first, then his law business, and finally golf. He hated practice and some years the only tournaments he played were the national championships he won.

Jones was a supremely natural player who swept serenely through the ball with a rhythmic swing whose lazy grace belied its power. His tee shots averaged 250 yards and for decades he was the only man ever to get home in two at the par five, 603-yard 17th hole of the Olympic Club in San Francisco. But Jones' true strengths were his surgically accurate irons and his touch with Calamity Jane, his simple blade putter.

Jones had already established himself as the best golfer in the world when, in 1930, he did the unthinkable: winning the Open and Amateur titles of America and Great Britain in one season.

It was a journey that began in St Andrews with the title Jones wanted most: the British Amateur. In three of a gruelling series of eight matches, Bobby squeezed through by 1-up. In the 36-hole final against England's Roger Wethered, he won by seven holes up with six to play.

Two weeks later, at Hoylake, Jones broke the competitive course record for 72 holes and won his third British Open by two strokes. No American had ever won both titles, and New Yorkers gave him a ticker-tape welcome home.

At the US Open at Interlachen, a 68 in round three gave him a five-stroke

◄ Bobby Jones: 'a phenomenal record, compiled while playing no more often than the average duffer'

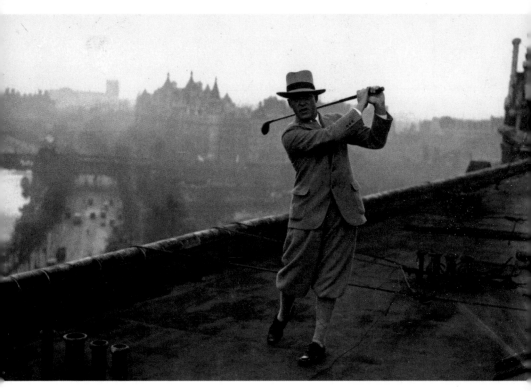

▲ 'Rhythmic swing whose lazy grace belied its power': Jones demonstrates on the Savoy Hotel's roof, London

lead. In the final round, Jones double-bogeyed three of the four par-three holes but, with trademark resilience, finished with birdies on three of his last six holes for a two-stroke victory.

His victory in the US Amateur at Merion seemed preordained. Jones was never down to an opponent and, in the 36-hole final, beat Eugene Homans by eight up with seven to play.

Bobby Jones was the epitome of modesty and grace, a Southern gentleman, revered above all of America's sportsmen, yet humble. At Harvard he was ineligible for the golf team, having already played at Georgia Tech so, at a time when he was US Open Champion, he served as the team's assistant manager. And his name was so synonymous with perfect behaviour that the USGA named its highest award for sportsmanship after him.

But his career was as brief as it was brilliant. Jones was only 28 when he completed the Grand Slam – and at that point, having achieved all of his goals, he retired.

He had plenty to keep him occupied. He published books, designed clubs for Spalding and collaborated with Warner Brothers on a series of instructional film shorts co-starring the likes of Jimmy Cagney and Edward G Robinson. But most of Jones' energy went into the pursuit of a dream.

In 1931 he and a group of investors purchased 365 acres near Augusta, Georgia, and in January 1933 the Augusta National opened for play.

The site offered rolling countryside planted with a dazzling assortment of trees, shrubs and flowers, with Georgia pines, azaleas and dogwoods prominent. Scottish architect Alister Mackenzie

◄ Friends and rivals: Bobby Jones (right) with Gene Sarazen

– whose designs include Australia's Royal Melbourne and Cypress Point in California, a 1928 creation considered to be among the world's top 10 courses – collaborated with Jones on the design.

Jones had two desires: that the course rise out of the terrain rather than be stamped on it, recalling the rolling feel of Scottish linksland; and that each hole offer alternative lines of attack, with the reward in proportion to the risk.

Augusta National's generous fairways, sparse bunkering and expansive greens gave it a wide-open, welcoming appearance. It looked easy but wasn't – exactly what Jones wanted.

After Augusta National opened, the USGA expressed interest in holding a US Open there, but the idea did not sit well with the club members. "If we're going to hold a tournament," they reasoned, "let's hold our own."

So in 1934 the Masters was born, with Jones as host. In those days it was called the Augusta National Invitation: an invitation from Jones to old compatriots and the best new players. It became something more when Jones was persuaded to come out of retirement and play, but his chipping and putting were not what the public had hoped for, and he finished the tournament in a tie for 13th place.

Nowhere did Jones enrapture fans more than at St Andrews. It was here that much of his career unfolded, from his first Open appearance in 1921 – when poor play led him to stomp off the course – to the Open he dominated from start to finish in 1927,

and his crowning achievement in the Amateur of 1930.

In 1936 he returned to the Old Course, unannounced, for a casual round. By the time he reached the first tee, 5,000 St Andreans were waiting to see him play. More than 20 years passed before Jones returned again, and when he did he was made a Freeman of the Royal Burgh of St Andrews.

Bobby Jones died in 1971, leaving a legacy like no other. His spirit lives on every year in the Masters, an event that has grown in leaps and bounds since 1934.

Gene Sarazen

And the biggest leap came one year after its inception, when Gene Sarazen fired "the shot heard round the world".

Sarazen was three strokes off the lead in the final round when he came to the 15th hole, a 500-yard par five. After his tee shot left him 230 yards from the hole, he elected to go for the green with a 4-wood.

The ball shot out low and straight at the flag, cleared the pond in front of the green, took one big bounce

◀ Bobby Jones in 1921, putting at the Amateur Golf Championship at Hoylake, where he later broke the course record

▲ Bobby Jones with the Claret Jug after winning the 1927 Open at St Andrews

and rolled straight into the cup for an albatross two.

Sarazen had made up all three strokes with one shot. He went on to par the last three holes and tie with Craig Wood, whom he trounced in a playoff.

Suddenly, the tournament had tradition and panache. Today, the Masters ranks with the Open, US Open and the PGA Championship as one of the four most coveted titles in golf. With his dramatic victory, Sarazen became the first man to win all four.

The son of Italian immigrants, Sarazen had learned the game as a caddie in suburban New York. In 1922, his name was etched on to the US Open trophy when he won by one stroke over Jones. Later that summer, at 20, he became the youngest PGA champion ever and in 1923 he made it two PGAs in a row.

But the success may have been too much too soon, and he fell into a decade of relative decline. In 1932, Sarazen decided his high scores had come largely from poor bunker play – so he invented the sand wedge.

Sarazen got his idea while flying: when the tail fins went down, the plane rose. Reasoning that if he could lower the sole of his niblick it would help lift the ball from sand, he soldered a thick flange on the back of the club, angled so that the flange hit the sand first, allowing the front of the club to bounce upward. Now he could hit behind the ball and splash it out.

At the Open in 1932 at Sandwich, Sarazen's new club saved him stroke after stroke and he won by five strokes, breaking the 72-hole record. Two weeks later, he won the US Open at Skokie Country Club.

At about the same time, another equipment development was occurring: the USGA and the Royal & Ancient had approved the production of golf clubs with tubular steel shafts. Clubmaking switched from a craft dependent on the skills of artisans to a purely mechanical process, and suddenly all clubs were created equal.

▼ Bobby Jones plays a mashie shot during the Open at St Andrews, 1927

THE ULTIMATE AMATEUR

▼ Inventive: Gene Sarazen in action

Up to this point, golfers had built up their arsenals haphazardly, buying a brassie here and a mashie there in the hope of assembling a collection of sticks with similar heft and flex. Often, the result was a bagful of weapons at odds with one another.

But steel shafts put an end to that with the advent of the matched set. Not only were the clubs consistent, but the lie of the clubhead and the flexibility of the shaft could be tailored to fit individual needs.

It was also at this time that golf clubs began to be designated with numbers instead of names – the spoon became a 3-wood, the mashie a 5-iron, the niblick a 9-iron – and for a while the numbers got out of hand. Lawson Little, the winner of back-to-back titles in the US and British Amateurs in 1934 and 1935, is reputed to have used no fewer than 31 clubs.

Something had to be done, so in 1938 the USGA limited the golfer's armaments to 14. The R&A followed a year later.

Four years later, a cap was imposed on the liveliness of the ball. The game's ruling bodies had limited the size and weight of the ball in the 1920s, but that hadn't stopped one manufacturer from creating a rocket that went 50 yards further than

anything else on the market.

What's more, as golfers began swinging their steel shafts with a vigour impossible in the hickory era, everyone from tour pros to grandmothers got extra distance. So, in 1942, the USGA imposed a limit on the velocity a golf ball may have at impact: 250ft per second.

▲ Seven-time major winner: Gene Sarazen with the Open trophy at Sandwich, 1932

An American Triumvirate

As golf equipment became more consistent, precise and powerful, so did the players, and in the late 1930s a new breed of strong and talented professionals came to the fore. Among them was England's answer to Bobby Jones, the legendary Henry Cotton.

Cotton was a sublime ball-striker and exceptionally long when he needed to be, because he had reserves of effortless power. This was due partly to good technique, but he was also very strong – one of his favourite drills was hitting 5-iron shots using just his left arm.

Cotton elevated the status of professional golfers, many of whom at that time were treated as second-class citizens: it was common for them not to be allowed in the clubhouse. Cotton would not stand for such nonsense and was not afraid to say as much. But he did not always endear himself to his fellow pros, often preferring not to mix with them. And he had a fiery temperament, kept under wraps during championships but often in evidence off the course.

But Cotton could be generous with his knowledge. In 1938, he travelled to St Andrews at his own expense to advise the Great Britain and Ireland Walker Cup team. The home side won the cup for the first time in its history.

Cotton won three Open Championships and his first, in 1934 at Sandwich, was perhaps his finest. Aged just 27, he produced world-class golf that blew everyone else into the weeds. Starting with a 67, he then shot a second-round 65 – a championship record score that stood for 43 years and inspired Dunlop to name the 65 ball. Only five golfers broke 70 in that Open and Cotton shot two of the rounds, giving him an unassailable nine-shot lead.

When he won the championship again in 1937, Cotton was at the height of his powers. He would surely have won several more Opens had World War II not intervened, and he had to wait until 1948 for his hat-trick.

By then he had turned 40 and knew it would probably be pretty much downhill after that – but he was still capable of winning well into the 1950s. He retired to his beloved Penina golf course in Portugal, where young pros flocked to meet him.

Across the pond, golf got another much-needed shot in the arm when America produced its own Great Triumvirate: Byron Nelson, Sam Snead and Ben Hogan.

Byron Nelson

All three were born in 1912, but it was Nelson, a lanky, baby-faced Texan, who first gained major attention when he won the 1937 Masters.

In the final round he was four strokes off the lead of Ralph Guldahl. But at Augusta's par-three 12th,

'Sublime ball striker': Henry Cotton, who demanded better treatment for golf professionals and wrote on the subject in newspapers and magazines

AN AMERICAN TRIUMVIRATE

Guldahl took a double-bogey five, then followed with a bogey at the par-five 13th. Nelson birdied the 12th and eagled the 13th, taking a two-stroke lead that he never relinquished.

Two years later, Nelson won the US Open in dramatic style, holing a 1-iron approach shot for eagle en route to a playoff victory. That iron was not unexpected, for no one since Harry Vardon had hit the ball with the accuracy of Lord Byron.

His key was a swing unlike all others, the first to adapt successfully to the steel-shafted club. While the rest of the world continued to imitate Bobby Jones, with little leg movement and a pivot against a tall and braced left side, Nelson put some action in his legs, let his left knee buckle, and dipped downward through impact.

However, he continued to use one element of the Jones swing – the straight left arm. Until that time, the left arm was allowed to bend on the backswing, to keep players' motion in sync with their wooden-shafted clubs. But if the shafts were firmer, so the leading arm could be, too. Nelson helped popularise the 'modern' swing, very similar to the one we use today.

By 1944, he had lifted a second Masters, the PGA and two dozen tour victories. In 1944 alone he won eight events, but he was about to climb even higher.

In 1945, Byron Nelson came as close as any golfer has come to being unbeatable. He won 18 of that year's

35 tournaments, 11 of them in one string; he finished second seven times; his scoring average was a phenomenal 68.33; and he finished every tournament under par.

At the end of the next season, with most of his ambitions fulfilled, Nelson retired and bought a Texas cattle ranch. Years later, he returned to the game as a TV commentator and host of the Byron Nelson Classic tournament.

Samuel Snead

When Nelson retired in 1946, aged 34, Samuel Jackson Snead was just getting warmed up. Although by 1945 he had three dozen victories under his belt, there were nearly 50 more wins ahead of him in a career that would last another 34 years and beyond.

Slammin' Sam came out of western Virginia with more raw talent than the

▲ Byron Nelson competing in the 1937 Ryder Cup at Royal Birkdale, which the USA won 8-4

AN AMERICAN TRIUMVIRATE

game had ever seen and with a swing as strong and graceful as the leap of a panther. In his first pro event, the 1936 Hershey Open, Sam belted two opening drives out of bounds. For his third attempt, he let his swing flow and drove the green, 350 yards away. With that shot, he arrived.

Snead won his first event later that year and the next year he won five more, the first instalments in a total of 84 victories – more than any man in history.

But in that same 1937 season, Snead finished second in the US Open despite a four-round total of 283, just one stroke off the tournament record. The only blemish on his career is his failure to win the US Open despite 37 tries, a dozen top-ten finishes and four times as runner-up.

Snead's most painful loss was to Byron Nelson in 1939 at the Spring Mill Country Club near Philadelphia, where a par five on his final hole would have taken the title. Thinking he needed a birdie, Snead stumbled to an eight.

He had another chance in 1947 at St Louis Country Club where, in a playoff with Lew Worsham, the two came to the 18th green still even and with both balls about 30in from the cup. Snead set up to putt first, but Worsham asked for a ruling. "That kind of rattled me," Snead said. He was, indeed, further away, and when he putted, he missed. Worsham made, for a one-stroke win.

In 1949, at Medinah, Snead needed pars on the last two holes but took three strokes from the edge of the 17th. And in 1953 at Oakmont, he entered the final round one shot behind Hogan; a final-round 76 left him six back.

But Snead recovered both his composure and his game. No entry in the record book is longer than his: among his seven dozen wins are three Masters, three PGAs and the 1946 Open, plus scores of lesser titles.

Age never seemed to slow Snead. In 1965 he won the Greater Greensboro

▼ Great Britain and Ireland benefiting from help from Henry Cotton: the Walker Cup at St Andrews, 1938

▲ The first golfer to win tournaments in six different decades: Sam Snead at Carnoustie, 1937

from over. When in 1980 he won the Commemorative, a Senior event, he became the first golfer to record victories in six different decades.

Ben Hogan

While Snead played golf naturally, Ben Hogan had to "dig it out of the dirt". Just 5ft 8.5in and under 10 stone, Hogan was the runt of the caddie pen at the Glen Garden Country Club near Fort Worth, where Byron Nelson also learned the game. In 1927, Bantam Ben lost the caddie championship to Nelson – and did not enjoy his first taste of defeat.

But there was more frustration to come. For the first several years of his career he fought a vicious hook, and he made three abortive attempts at the pro circuit before achieving modest success in 1937. It was another three years before he broke through with his first victory at the Pinehurst North-South. By that time, Nelson and Snead had won 30 tournaments.

becoming, at 52 years and 10 months, the oldest player ever to win on the USPGA Tour. And he tied for third in the 1974 USPGA Championship – at the age of 62!

But his competitive days were far

But Hogan won in each of the two weeks following Pinehurst, taking four tournaments in all, and finished the season as the leading money winner. In 1941 and 1942 he continued the domination, piling up a dozen more victories.

Hogan served two years in the Army Air Corps before his discharge in the summer of 1945. Once back, he wasted no time, winning five events by the end of the year. Then, in 1946, he put together a season nearly as overpowering as Nelson's in 1945: of the 32 events he entered, Hogan won 13, finished second in six and third in three.

Among the tournaments he won was his first major championship – the USPGA – and among those he almost won were the Masters and the US Open. In both of those two, a missed putt at the final hole cost him the title.

Hogan was never able to master the putting game, but he came as close as anyone to mastering golf from tee to green. He claimed he preferred practice to play and, through relentless pursuit of improvement, banished his hook in favour of a fade.

In 1947, Hogan again led the Tour in victories with seven, and in 1948 he added 10 more, including a second USPGA Championship and his first US Open. Eight months later, he was lucky to be alive.

In February, his car collided head-on with a Greyhound bus and he broke a collarbone, fractured his pelvis, crushed an ankle and suffered massive internal

▼ Ben Hogan: a master of golf from tee to green

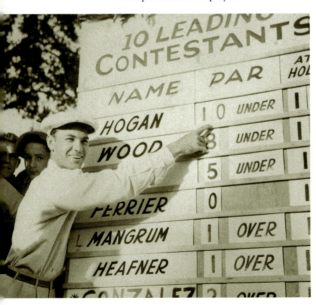

▼ Winner: Ben Hogan points to his winning score of 10 under par at the Chicago Open at Elmhurst Country Club in 1941

injuries. Doctors said he might never walk again, but by August Hogan was swinging a club and by December he was on the course.

The following January, he returned to the site of his US Open victory, Riviera, for a comeback. Incredibly, he shot 73-69-69-69, and appeared to have won before Sam Snead tied him and then prevailed in a playoff.

At the US Open at Merion, visibly in pain from walking a 36-hole final day, Hogan managed to tie Lloyd Mangrum and George Fazio in regulation play, then beat them the next day in an 18-hole playoff.

Thereafter, Hogan concentrated on the majors, winning his first Masters in 1951 and in the same year taking the US Open at Oakland Hills, over a set-up considered the most severe test ever.

But Hogan's vintage year was 1953, during which he won the Masters, the US Open and the British Open inside 12 weeks. At Augusta, he won with a 284 that lowered the tournament record by five. At Oakmont, he led from wire to wire to take the US Open.

Then, persuaded to play the Open for the first time, he spent a week learning about linksland golf and assaulted the course at Carnoustie. With a course-record 68 in the final round, he won by four strokes and became the first player to win the Masters and the US and British Opens in the same year.

Hogan won nine major championships, and his name remains a symbol of courage, dedication and indomitable spirit. And for many golfers it also means hope – of improving their swing. For years there were rumours of a 'secret', and in 1955, Hogan confessed to Life magazine that he 'cupped' the left wrist just before reaching the top of the backswing.

In 1957, in Five Lessons: The Modern Fundamentals of Golf, written with Herbert Warren Wind,

he described the 'pronation' of the wrists as well as the importance of the left hip turning out of the way on the downswing to generate power.

And he introduced a new image: he visualised a pane of glass that ran from the ball up through the shoulders and indicated the proper plane of the swing. His ideas are still being debated, and tried.

▲ Giving hope to the gallery: Ben Hogan plays a tee shot during the 1956 Canada Cup at Wentworth, won by the Hogan-Snead duo for the US

The Ladies' Game

▼ Swinging in silk: an advertisement for women's golf fashions in 1910

NEW SILK :: SPORTS COATS

Registered design (*as sketch*), the most useful garment imaginable, beautifully made from rich quality, double-combed silk, extra bright finish, combining the fit of a perfectly made tailor coat with the comfort and warmth of a throw-on. A dainty and most becoming garment, stocked in more than 100 fashionable shades.

33 inches long, 63/-
36 " " 72/6
44 " " 94/6
Silk cap to match, 21/-
SENT ON APPROVAL

Debenham & Freebody

Wigmore Street (Cavendish Sq.), London, W.

Famous over a Century for Taste, for Quality, for Value.

Ever since Mary Queen of Scots, women all over the world have embraced the game of golf. It wasn't until the mid-19th century, however, that the first ladies' clubs were formed.

At that time, restrictive clothing made it impossible for women to exploit their talents fully. It was even considered unladylike to swing the club above shoulder height, and the women's game was unlikely to take off in a big way. Things changed, though. The Ladies' Golf Union was formed in 1893 and by the early 1900s, women's golf was in good health on both sides of the Atlantic.

But it was not very profitable. While the era of Ben Hogan, Byron Nelson and Sam Snead transformed big-time golf into a game strictly for professionals, the top women players remained amateur until after World War II. This is not to say that there weren't some very fine women golfers. Two were downright magnificent.

During the 1920s, Joyce Wethered ruled Britannia with a graceful, compact swing and a buoyant temperament. In one incident at Sheringham, she putted out while a train thundered past 30 feet away. After securing victory, she was asked if the train hadn't put her off. Her reply: "what train?"

Wethered won four British Amateurs and five consecutive English Amateurs before retiring at 28. Bobby Jones called her the finest golfer – man or woman – he had ever seen.

Her last British Amateur title, in 1929, came with a two-up victory over the other powerhouse of women's golf, America's Glenna Collett. No woman in the US was a match for Glenna, who dominated the US Amateur with a record six victories, including three in a row from 1928–30, along with dozens of lesser events.

Her single frustration was in never winning the British Amateur, but when Margaret and Harriott Curtis, a pair of

▲ Imperturbable: Joyce Wethered with the Ladies' Amateur Championship trophy, St Andrews, 1929

► Model professional: Babe Zaharias with Wilson golf clubs after signing a $100,000 contract with the company, late 1940s

former US Amateur Champions from Boston, donated a cup for competition between America and Great Britain & Ireland, Glenna got a measure of satisfaction. The Curtis Cup was born, and Glenna was on the first six, undefeated US teams.

The 1946 US Amateur and 1947 British Amateur titles went to a Texan woman who changed the face of women's golf. Her name was Mildred, but everyone knew her as Babe.

Babe Didrikson was famous before she found celebrity as a golfer. She won gold in the javelin and 80-metre hurdles at the 1932 Olympics, and she was gifted at everything she tried: basketball, swimming, diving, rifle shooting, bowling, figure skating, bike racing and tennis. She even dabbled in baseball and football. But golf became her true love, and it soon outshone all her other sporting achievements combined.

The first formal round she played, she shot 93 while slugging out 250-yard tee shots. In 1935, she won the first important tournament she entered, the Texas Women's Amateur Championship.

Babe brought a new work ethic to

women's golf: learning from Tommy Armour, the finest teacher of the time, she played and practised up to 16 hours a day. Her first years were spent touring in exhibitions with top men professionals, and later with her husband, professional wrestler George Zaharias. A born entertainer, when asked how a slender woman of 5ft 7in could hit the ball so far, she said, "I just hitch up my girdle and give it a rip."

Her exhibitions made her a professional in the eyes of the USGA, but by 1944 she was reinstated as an amateur and wasted no time in winning the 1946 US Women's Amateur and the 1947 British Amateur at Gullane.

The Babe then turned pro again, and made the astute decision to acquire the services of agent Fred Corcoran. That same year, she signed a contract with Wilson Sporting Goods for $100,000. But what the Babe really wanted was serious competition and an audience.

So in 1950, the Ladies Professional Golf Association was formed in the US, with 11 women as its charter members. Corcoran stage-managed the tour and Wilson paid the bills, but the women kept the books, handled the correspondence and called their own rulings.

The Babe dominated the early years, racking up an astonishing

▼ All-round athlete: Babe Zaharias excelled in many sports

THE LADIES' GAME

31 tournament victories. And she probably would have won dozens more events had her career not been curtailed by cancer.

She was diagnosed in 1953, but a mere 14 weeks later she was back on the course, and the next year she won five tournaments. Three more victories came in 1955, but then the cancer returned. In 1956, Babe Zaharias died at the tragically young age of 42.

But Babe was not the only talent on that fledgling women's tour. Even on her best days, she could be beaten by the freckle-faced Patty Berg.

By the age of 16, Patty had won the Minneapolis City Golf Championship and a year later she nearly won the US Amateur, a title she later went on to claim along with 28 others.

During the war she served in the women's Marines, then came out firing as a professional golfer with a victory in the first Women's US Open in 1946. Along with Babe, Berg – who was the LPGA's first president – dominated women's pro golf for the next decade, amassing 44 wins.

The two other top-notch players at the dawn of the LPGA were Louise Suggs and Betsy Rawls. Suggs developed such clubhead speed that people called her the female Ben Hogan. Before turning pro she won the US and British

Open, in 1954, but in the decade that followed, Mickey Wright set a new standard in women's pro golf. Shy and retiring, she delivered in game what she lacked in glamour, with a swing that is to this day called the finest golf has produced.

From 1957 until 1965 there was no one who could touch Mickey. Over that span she won 65 tournaments, nearly a third of those she entered. In 1961, she won 10 events including the US Open, the LPGA Championship

◄ The LPGA's first president: Patty Berg drives off at Sandy Lodge, 1936

▼ US Open winner: Betsy Rawls, pictured in 1952

Amateurs, then added two US Opens and an LPGA Championship, among 50 career victories.

Rawls joined the tour in 1951, won her first US Open the same year and added 54 other events. Only one other player has won the Women's US Open four times: Mickey Wright.

She finished fourth in her first

▶ The first million-dollar woman golfer: Kathy Whitworth in action in August 1975

and her own Mickey Wright Open in her hometown of San Diego. She followed with 10 more wins in 1962, a record 13 in 1963 and 11 in 1964.

The rise of Mickey Wright mirrored the growth of the LPGA, which in turn reflected the good times. After two decades of depression and war, new courses were popping up everywhere in the US and Britain. They weren't quite like the old ones.

Earth-moving equipment had replaced horse-drawn scrapers and riding mowers had made courses easier to maintain, while also producing mammoth greens and tees.

The prominent architects of the 20s and 30s had passed away, but into the breach had stepped Robert Trent Jones. A fine amateur player, Jones became the first man to train specifically as a golf course architect. At Cornell University he devised his own curriculum, combining landscape design and agronomy, and it was he who, in 1993, designed the LPGA's home course at Daytona, Florida.

Mickey Wright's retirement had left a void in women's golf. But one discovery was Texan Kathy Whitworth, who led the LPGA money list eight times between 1965 and 1973. No player has amassed more official victories than Whitworth, who totalled 88 wins and became the first woman golfer to pass one million dollars in official prize winnings.

In a similar milestone to Whitworth's, American Judy Rankin broke the $100,000 barrier for a single season when in 1976 she won seven events.

Then there was long-hitting JoAnne Carner. She didn't turn pro until she was 30, but in the decade and half starting in 1970 she won 42 LPGA titles, while adding a dash of

colour to women's golf.

In 1975, New York marketing mogul Ray Volpe took over as commissioner of the LPGA, and under his seven-year leadership the tour's purses quadrupled while the televised events jumped from two to 14. More talented women began to join the LPGA Tour, and one of them, Nancy Lopez from New Mexico, became the LPGA's first superstar with a

◀ Solheim Cup-winning captain: JoAnne Carner with the trophy at the Greenbrier, White Sulphur Springs, West Virginia in 1994

▲ Nancy Lopez: the LPGA's first superstar

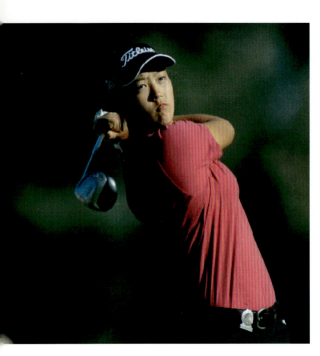

▲ Prodigy: the 13-year-old Michelle Wie in 2003

winning 50 tournaments, and Lopez remained the LPGA Tour's marquee attraction for 20 years. But at the same time, the supporting cast became stronger as players such as Pat Bradley, Beth Daniel, Amy Alcott, Patty Sheehan and Betsy King took women's pro golf to a new level.

The LPGA began billing itself "the best women golfers in the world", and for a long time after the turn of the century Sweden's Annika Sorenstam was the dominant player in a tour that has expanded to include events in Canada, England, Australia, Japan and South Korea. Sorenstam won a record-threatening 72 LPGA titles, including 10 majors, before calling it a day in 2008.

Nowadays, most eyes are on the Mexican Lorena Ochoa who, having been ranked the world's top woman golfer in the three years up to May 2010, is now regarded as the best player – of either gender – in her country's history.

They start 'em young in Guadalajara. Lorena, having picked up a golf club at the age of five, won her first state event when she was six and had claimed her first national title by the time she was seven. She was clearly bound for the

phenomenal rookie year.

She scored back-to-back early-season victories and then won the next five events she entered – including the LPGA Championship. That season, Lopez won nine times and established a new scoring average.

From there she just got better,

LPGA Tour, which she joined in 2003, and had made her mark with 27 wins, including two majors, by 2010.

Women's golf in Europe

experienced difficult times in the 80s and 90s, but it is now capitalising on the success of some of the continent's finest players – who also happen to be some of the world's best.

For years the Women's British Open struggled to assert itself, until finally it was awarded major status. With that came big prize money, and the Women's British Open is assured of a world class gathering of talent every year.

As is Solheim Cup week. This event, launched in 1990, is essentially the women's equivalent of the Ryder Cup, contested biennially between the leading professionals in Europe and the United States.

Thirty or 40 years ago, the tournament – named after Karsten Solheim, the founder of the Ping golf company – might have been a walkover for the US. As it was, its launch coincided with a period when European golf was thriving as never before.

In Laura Davies, Europe has had one of the world's best golfers – and certainly one of the most exciting to watch. Her hero is Seve Ballesteros, so it's no coincidence that she plays like him. She exploded on to the scene in

▼ Get in: Laura Davies celebrates after birdying the second hole during the second Solheim Cup, at Dalmahoy, Scotland in 1992. Europe beat the USA to tie the series

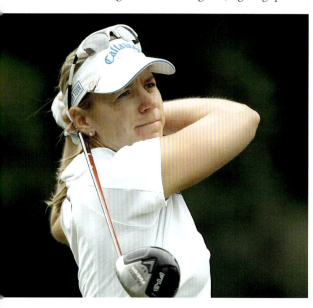

the mid-1980s, thumping drives in a fashion that set her apart from any other golfer of her generation.

Although she is near the end of her career, there is still no greater treat than watching Davies unleash a drive with seemingly no regard for the consequences. To go with the power, though, she has a strong all-round game and a courageous, fighting spirit.

She has won the Ladies' European Tour Order of Merit seven times – a record – and has clocked up an extraordinary 78 pro wins throughout the world. That number includes 20 wins on the LPGA and four major titles.

While Laura was still at her inspired best, along came the contrasting persona of Annika Sorenstam. Her diminutive frame and unassuming manner hid one of the greatest women's golf talents of all time.

Quiet, softly spoken, but a clinical winning machine, Annika was leading individual in the 1992 World Amateur Team Championship and blitzed the collegiate world while at the University of Arizona.

After turning pro, she won the Rookie of the Year title in 1993 in Europe and claimed the same title in the US in 1995, a year in which she became the first player to top the European and LPGA Tour money lists in the same season. That year she also won her first US Open.

Sorenstam could produce explosive streaks of low scoring, yet she did not suffer the dips in form that so many golfers endure. There have been few players, male or female, who have made fewer mistakes than Annika. She had a good technique and swung the club with a beautiful, smooth rhythm. She hit almost every fairway and green and she putted like an angel. To cap it all, she had an unflappable, nerveless disposition.

Together, Annika and Laura spearheaded Europe's challenge in the early years of the Solheim Cup. The inaugural contest in 1990, at Lake Nona in Florida, witnessed a powerful performance from the United States. But two years later at Dalmahoy in Scotland, Europe turned the tables. Leading by one point after the first two days, the home side routed the supposedly stronger Americans in the singles matches by 7–3.

The 2003 European team pulled off a resounding, seven-point win in Sweden but their transatlantic rivals have held sway in recent tournaments. The 2011 event, to be held at Killeen Castle in Ireland, has all the makings of a cracker.

Like the men's professional game, women's golf has changed beyond all recognition in the last 100 years. But it's never looked in better health.

◀ 'Unflappable, nerveless disposition': Annika Sorenstam holds the winner's trophy for the 1996 US Women's Open at Pine Needles, North Carolina

The Big Three

To most people, the name of George S May does not mean a thing in the context of golf's Big Three – Arnold Palmer, Jack Nicklaus and Gary Player. But this flamboyant Chicago businessman played a pivotal role: he launched the era of televised golf.

And what a moment May chose to put golf on TV. In 1953, for the final round of the World Championship of Golf, he positioned a single camera atop the grandstand at the 18th green of the Tam O'Shanter Country Club in Michigan.

Lew Worsham needed a birdie three to reach a playoff for the record $25,000 first prize and faced a wedge approach of 120 yards. His low shot hit well short of the pin but rolled and rolled – nearly 60 feet – and dropped in for an eagle two and outright victory.

That magic moment, witnessed by a million viewers, changed everything. The US Open came to TV in 1954, the Masters in 1955, and by the early 60s every significant tournament was either on screen or trying to get there.

Arnold Palmer

Golf's first TV star made his entrance in the form of Western Pennsylvania's Arnold Daniel Palmer: the classic American hero, with a swaggering gait, a ready smile and the shoulders of an NFL fullback.

Arnold was three when he first picked up a club. At seven he broke a hundred, at 14 he shot 71, and by the time he entered Wake Forest University he had won just about every school, county and state-wide event.

The Palmer swing was less than elegant, but he pulverised the ball. His putting was equally ungraceful, but he rapped it home from everywhere. He had a burning will to win and the perfect psyche for golf – a fighting spirit without a temper. His go-for-broke style sometimes got him in trouble, but his resourcefulness usually got him out.

He didn't play a golf course; he beat it into submission.

A victory in the 1954 US Amateur persuaded him to turn pro, and four years later he won the first of four Masters titles along with four other events. But it was in 1960 that Arnold Palmer truly began his reign.

That April he arrived at Augusta with four wins in his pocket. A first-round 67 gave him the Masters lead, and he held on to it until the final moments on Sunday, when Ken Venturi pulled in front. Palmer came to the last two holes needing two birdies to win, and he got them both. The Palmer Charge was born. Six weeks later it became legendary.

By the start of the final round of the US Open at the Cherry Hills Country Club, he was seven strokes off the lead. But at the par-four first, Palmer drove the green, 346 yards away. Then his two-putt birdie ignited the most explosive stretch of sub-par golf the US Open had seen – four birdies in a row, six in the first seven holes – for an outward-nine score of 30. Suddenly, Arnie was tied for the lead, and he closed with a seven-under- par 65 for a

◀ 'A swaggering gait, a ready smile and the shoulders of an NFL full-back': Arnold Palmer in 1953

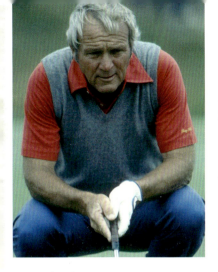

Between 1960 and 1970, golf boomed in the United States. The number of players doubled from five million to ten, and the number of courses exploded from 6,300 to 10,000. But no aspect of the game grew more dramatically than the professional tour.

Except for the major championships and a couple of California pro-ams, the tour had for years been a succession of modest, community-run tournaments. But as TV networks and sponsors began to pay serious money, pro golf became big business.

The growth did not come without pain. For a time, a conflict brewed between the PGA of America, the sponsors and the players over who should receive the lion's share of broadcast fees. So the players split from their teaching-pro brethren in the PGA, taking most of the rights money with them. USGA executive director Joseph C Dey took over as the first commissioner of the organisation that became known as the PGA Tour.

In 1958, the total purse for the tour had been one million dollars. A decade later, when the PGA Tour was formed, the purses increased to five million.

◄◄ 'When Arnie was happy, he grinned': Palmer celebrates after sinking a long putt

◄ 'He rapped it home from everywhere': Palmer lines up a putt during the 1981 Open at Royal St George's

two-stroke victory.

When Arnie was happy, he grinned; when he was unhappy, he grimaced – and fans celebrated and suffered with him. They celebrated four Masters and they suffered three playoff losses in the US Open. They celebrated back-to-back victories in the Open Championship and they suffered as he struggled to win the USPGA.

In all, Arnold Palmer won 60 US events, and another 29 around the world. He led the money list four times, was the first player to win $100,000 in a single season and the first to reach a million dollars in career earnings. And no player has been loved so much by so many.

Jack Nicklaus

That era produced a legion of talented young players, but one rose above them all: Jack Nicklaus.

When he came to golf, the chunky 10-year-old from Columbus, Ohio had, in Charlie Nicklaus, a devoted father who loved the game; in Scioto Country Club a home course that had hosted a US Open; and in club pro Jack Grout one of the finest instructors.

But most of all, Jack Nicklaus had raw talent. He shot 51 for the first nine holes he played. By 13 he had broken 70 at Scioto, and at 16 he won the Ohio State Open.

Jack's first step toward immortality came in the 1959 US Amateur Championship, where he scored an 18th-hole victory in the final match. Two years later he won the Amateur and NCAA titles, and the year after that he joined the pro tour.

No player was more eagerly anticipated, and yet none was more rudely greeted. They called him Fat Jack and Nick Louse, said he was too young, too heavy, too sombre, too slow – but the truth was, he wasn't Arnold Palmer.

Where Palmer warmed to the galleries, Nicklaus ignored them. While Palmer could turn an ordinary round into high drama, Jack made superb play look matter-of-fact. His drives were gargantuan, his irons majestic and

Jack's rookie year, in the US Open at Oakmont. In the heart of Palmer country, the man treated Arnie's Army to four days of gallant golf. His 283 put him in first place – in a tie with Nicklaus. In the playoff, Jack took the lead at the first hole, never let go and was ahead by three strokes at the end.

He won twice more before the end of that year, then in 1963 exploded for five wins, including the Masters and the USPGA. The 23-year-old Nicklaus remained the man to beat for the next quarter century.

Jack managed his practice and play to peak for the Masters, the US Open, the Open and the USPGA. When he won the 1966 Open he became, at 26, the youngest man to complete the career Grand Slam. And that was just the beginning.

Ultimately, Nicklaus won 18 major championships – six Masters, five USPGAs, four US Opens and three Opens – a record that no other player could approach until Tiger Woods came along. He did not simply win; he won in commanding, occasionally superhuman style. His victory in the 1965 Masters came by nine strokes with

◀ 'Making superb play look matter-of-fact': Jack Nicklaus takes a swing during the 1969 Open at Royal Lytham & St Annes

he putted with the touch of an angel, but he went about his business with plodding monotony.

The inevitable Palmer-Nicklaus showdown came halfway through a then-record score of 271.

At one time or another, Nicklaus held or shared the 18-hole and 72-hole scoring records for each of the four major championships. Five times he won two majors in the same year, and in 1972 he came within a whisker of

duplicating Ben Hogan's Triple Crown.

But Nicklaus didn't always have it all his own way. Lee Trevino, with six majors, was one of a handful of players who were able occasionally to put a dent in his challenge.

A world-class ball striker and effervescent character, Trevino won only two Open Championships, but he won them back to back. At Birkdale in 1971, he held his nerve on the back nine to edge out Nicklaus. The next year at Muirfield, Trevino succeeded in stopping Nicklaus in his tracks.

Gary Player

A more enduring challenge than Trevino's came from the Man in Black: Gary Player, the South African who in the 1960s ranked alongside Nicklaus and Palmer.

No golfer has won more events worldwide – 184 at the last count. Nine of those wins were majors, and when he won the 1965 US Open at Hazeltine, Player joined Hogan and Sarazen in a club that would soon include Nicklaus as the only players to complete a modern Grand Slam of vicperformance that he could afford a double-bogey six on the final hole.

Perhaps the greatest of his Open wins involved a classic battle with Nicklaus at Carnoustie in 1968. The fairway wood shot Player hit over bunkers on the par-five 14th to within two feet of the hole, giving him an eagle three, was one of the most timely shots in championship history.

When he won his second USPGA title at Oakland Hills, Player thumped his ball out of thick rough to within tapping-in distance. It was executed at exactly the right time, and is considered one of the greatest ever wedge shots.

At times, Player could charge just as well as Arnold Palmer – a fact that was never more evident than at the 1978 Masters. Aged 43, he was trailing the leaders by some distance going into the final round, but he dug deep and birdied seven of his final 10 holes for an astonishing eight-under-par 64 that took the

◀ Gary Player: 'gutsy, determined and able to get the job done when it mattered'

▼ Player watches a shot in 1978

tories. Woods has since joined them.

Gary Player was the template on which the modern golfer is based, eating bananas when virtually everyone else was smoking and pumping weights when everyone else thought he was mad. And he had a great temperament – gutsy, determined and able to get the job done when it mattered.

Player won Open Championships in three different decades. His first, at Muirfield in 1959, was such a dominant

THE BIG THREE

▼ 'No such thing as a lost cause': Gary Player plays in the Daks Tournament at Wentworth

title by one stroke.

That summed up Player's attitude: there was no such thing as a lost cause. In his semi-final against Tony Lema in the 1965 World Matchplay Championship, Player came back from seven down at halfway to tie after 36

holes, and win on the first playoff hole.

Player, the originator of the phrase "the more I practise, the luckier I get", wasn't lucky at all. He had great skill and, while not possessing a flawless technique, he was immensely strong and made the best of his talent. He was a fine mid-iron player and pitcher, an aggressive chipper and putter and probably the greatest bunker player ever.

Next on the scene to challenge Nicklaus was a new generation. Johnny Miller, the Californian who burst to prominence with a 63 in the final round of the 1973 US Open, went on to win two dozen events including the 1976 Open at Birkdale, where he thwarted the challenge of Nicklaus and the youthful Seve Ballesteros.

Next to step up was Kansas City's Tom Watson. His five Open Championships included a thrilling tussle with Nicklaus at Turnberry in 1977, Jack shooting rounds of 66-66 on Saturday and Sunday to fall one short of Watson's 66-65. Remembered by many as the greatest Open of all time, it was capped by a putt from Jack that travelled the width of the final green, dropping in for an improbable birdie three after he'd driven into gorse bushes. But Watson had played a marvellous approach and had only a three-footer to take the title.

That spurred Watson on to more daring deeds. Earlier that year he'd won his first Masters. In the 1981 Masters, he stared down Jack again and by the end was slipping on the Green Jacket for the second time. And at the 1982 US Open at Pebble Beach, Watson holed a chip shot out of deep rough beside the 71st green, giving him the birdie he needed for victory.

But when Jack lost, he lost graciously – and he always came back. Nicklaus was winning majors before Player, Trevino, Miller and Watson came along, and he was winning them after they stopped. His last hurrah came in the 1986 Masters, when he had not won a tournament in two years.

With nine holes to go, the 46-year-old Nicklaus, five strokes off the lead, summoned nine holes of the most electrifying golf the game has seen, blitzing through the back nine in 30 strokes and roaring past his young rivals to a one-stroke victory and a record sixth Green Jacket.

▲ Gary Player: 'The more I practise, the luckier I get'

Nicklaus' career is incomparable. No one has won more Masters, US Opens or USPGAs, and although others have won more Open Championships, no one can match Jack's seven runner-up finishes to go with his three victories. Along with his 18 championship titles, Jack finished second in the majors no fewer than 19 times.

Until Tiger Woods manages to surpass Nicklaus' majors record, there is no point anyone wasting their breath in debate. Nicklaus is still the greatest.

The Famous Five

The twelve months spanning April 1957 to March 1958 was perhaps the most significant year in the history of European golf. Within that year five bouncing babies – Severiano Ballesteros, Nick Faldo, Sandy Lyle, Bernhard Langer and Ian Woosnam – came into this world.

Within a couple of decades, they had transformed the face of European golf. Here's how the 'Famous Five' did it.

Severiano Ballesteros

It is fitting that Seve should be the oldest of the group, for it was he, born for such a role, who led the European charge.

It is impossible to exaggerate Seve's explosive impact on the game in the late 1970s. As if his good looks and film star smile were not enough to grab attention, he played golf like his life depended on every swashbuckling swing.

At the age of just 19, in 1976, Seve almost won the Open Championship at Birkdale, just losing out to Johnny Miller. The chip-and-run shot that he threaded through bunkers on the 72nd green, to save par and tie second, was labelled "the shot that was heard around the world", and it was an emphatic statement of intent. By the end of that year, Seve had topped the European Money List, as he did the following two years before heading to the US.

By that time, he was Open Champion, after a daredevil last round at Royal Lytham had snatched the trophy from under Hale Irwin's nose. Seve smashed drives to every corner of the course, yet kept making pars and the occasional birdie.

Some American journalists said he'd never win the US Masters because of his driving, but it wasn't nearly as wild as they thought. Seve was a smart thinker who knew what he was doing, and he was also a genius. He won the 1980 Masters like he was strolling in the park.

Seve's game was made for Augusta. There was more room off the tee than at most other championships, and no rough to speak of, so he could smash his driver as hard as he liked. At the time, he was one of the game's

▲ Severiano Ballesteros in the sandhills of Royal Birkdale, 1976 longest hitters and Augusta's slick, sloping greens placed huge emphasis on the short game skills in which Seve was king.

As a boy he'd taught himself to play with a 3-iron and pebbles on the beach, so chipping for real must have seemed easy. He won his second green jacket in 1983, and everyone thought he'd go on to win more. But he never won the Masters again.

Indeed, from the age of 31, Seve did not win another major. Someone with that much talent should have got his hands on more major trophies than his total of five.

Seve was never the most consistent of golfers, even in his prime, so when his game started to go off the boil when he was in his late thirties, everyone thought, "oh, he'll soon be back". But he never has been back, not really, and the golf world held its breath when it heard news of Seve's battle against a brain tumour in 2008. He's still showing his fighting mettle.

Nick Faldo

Next into this world was Nick Faldo, on 18 July 1957. Thirty years later, he stood triumphant at Muirfield celebrating his first major victory, the Open Championship.

He quickly added two more Opens, interspersed with three Masters wins, and his tally of six majors is evidence of his right to be described as Britain's greatest golfer.

Faldo and golf didn't meet until after his 14th birthday, but within four years he was English Amateur champion. He turned professional a year later, and soon won his first pro tournament, catapulting himself into the 1977 Ryder Cup team. This was when the golfing world started to take notice of Nick Faldo.

Playing with Peter Oosterhuis in the first-day fourballs and foursomes, he won both matches, with Jack Nicklaus and Ray Floyd among the scalps. In the final day singles he came up against Tom Watson, newly crowned Open Champion, and beat him too. Still only 20, Faldo didn't mind giving the world's best golfers a thrashing.

Faldo was a long hitter and his elegant, upright swing produced towering iron shots. He had a sweet short game and could putt the lights out when the mood took him. He became a winning machine – and then he decided he needed an overhaul, with David Leadbetter the mechanic.

After a couple of years in which he got to grips with his new swing, Faldo emerged better in every way. His ball-striking reached near perfection and he

▲ Britain's greatest golfer? Nick Faldo at the age of 21

▲ Winner of six majors: Nick Faldo with the Open trophy after winning in 1990 at St Andrews

minded approach and seeming lack of personality left him open to potshots, and for years he endured a fractious relationship with the media. But in the late 1990s Faldo's golf was not what it had once been, the newspapers softened up on him and we saw the softer side of Nick.

Now he can look back with satisfaction on a career record of nine PGA tour victories and 30 on the European Tour.

Bernhard Langer

In the early 1970s, teaching guru John Jacobs was talking to a German teaching professional about a young assistant pro he had working for him. "He is the most incredible ball-striker," enthused the teaching pro, "but he's an absolutely terrible putter." The teenager's name was Bernhard Langer.

Langer was for a long time one of Europe's best ball-strikers and shot-makers, but no one has suffered more agony on the greens. Since turning pro at an age when most youngsters are still at school, Langer has had to fight a golfer's worst affliction – the yips.

seemed mentally stronger, and for six or seven years, Faldo was the dominant golfer in the world.

No one else prepared so fastidiously for championships as Nick, and once on the course he withdrew into a cocoon of concentration. This single-

It's a psychological condition with physical effects: the muscles behave as if with a will of their own, making holing putts a nightmare. Traditionally, the yips hit golfers late in their careers; the fact that Langer had to deal with them pretty much from day one, and was phenomenally successful, tells you a lot about the rest of his game.

Amazingly, though, Langer was mostly a very good putter. He won two Masters on the fastest, scariest greens in the world, and got the ball in the hole often enough to stay at the top in Europe for a long time.

To do so, he had to resort to unorthodox methods. At first, he sought solutions with a change of equipment, but soon switched from an orthodox putting stroke to a cross-handed grip, with the left hand below the right. That worked fine – he won the US Masters in 1985, holding off Seve Ballesteros.

But the yips came back, so he found another method, clamping his left wrist against the putter shaft, clasping his forearm with his left hand. The putts started dropping again but once more, the yips returned. So, finally, Langer

went to the broomhandle putter.

Bernhard possesses an inner strength, thanks to his deeply held religious

▼ Bernhard Langer: 'the most incredible ball-striker'

▼ Bernhard Langer (right) with Ben Crenshaw after the 1985 Masters

faith, hard work and determination. Most pros, given similar turmoil on the greens, would have settled for making a living from teaching. But Langer kept on playing.

If his career seems to be defined by his troubles with the 'short stick', that does not do the man credit. Very few players have been able to sustain the high quality of golf that Langer did from 1972, when he turned pro. If you factor his troubles on the greens into his tally of more than 60 wins around the world and two Masters titles, it's a spectacular achievement.

Langer commands respect and affection both sides of the fairway ropes. A man of integrity and manners, he was the model Ryder Cup captain in 2004, when he guided Europe to victory by a record margin.

Sandy Lyle

Nick Faldo beat Sandy Lyle into this world by five months, but when it came to golf there was a time when it seemed Lyle would pip Faldo to the post in almost everything they did.

But then he did get a head start: by the time he was 14, Lyle was hitting 600 balls a day. He played for England boys at 14 and was English Amateur champion at

17 and 19, and this effortless momentum carried on into his pro career.

This is when Lyle and Faldo started to dovetail. Sandy won the Open at Royal St George's in 1985; Nick won it at Muirfield two years later. Sandy won the US Masters in 1988 (the first Brit to do so); Nick won it a year later. The pair were at the heart of Europe's Ryder Cup renaissance when, under the leadership of Tony Jacklin, they played like the world-beaters they were.

During the mid-1980s, Sandy seemed unstoppable, with the game to win wherever he teed it up. In an era when driver clubheads were made of timber, he could launch the ball distances that would be considered long even today. And his prowess with a 1-iron is legendary; he was quite simply the best in the world.

Allied to that power, Sandy had a soft touch on and around the greens. And even if he did drop a shot or two, he produced so many stunning strokes that he always gave himself birdie and eagle opportunities.

At the end of the 1980s and into the 1990s, the careers of Lyle and Faldo went their separate ways. As Faldo went

from strength to strength with his new swing, Sandy's game started to fall apart. Maybe over the years the bad shots chipped away at his inner self-belief, maybe Sandy just forgot how to play well. Whatever, within three years of

▲ He seemed unstoppable in the mid-1980s: Sandy Lyle kisses the Claret Jug after winning the 1985 Open at Royal St Georges

▲ Still a wonderful golfer to watch: Sandy Lyle in action in 2006

bloke with the laid-back nature reaped a handsome trophy harvest during his glittering career: 18 wins on the European Tour and six PGA Tour victories.

Ian Woosnam

Ian Woosnam is the baby of Europe's Famous Five. Not that this had anything to do with him being the last to win a European Tour event. The fact is, Woosie was a late developer.

He turned pro around the same time as the rest, but while they got on with the business of winning, Woosie struggled, forced to travel in a camper van eating baked beans out of a tin.

Woosnam was born on the English side of the border, to Welsh parents. He learned to play on a course that had 15 holes in Wales and three in England, so it's fitting that he should fly the flag for Wales.

Although not tall, Woosnam developed a strong physique, was a powerful ball-striker and had an admired swing. It seems amazing that he took so long to break through, but he had to go three times to the

winning the Masters he was a shadow of his former self.

Nevertheless, this talented, amiable

the main tour to retain his card. Once he had a foothold, though, Woosie made great strides.

He wasn't out of the money list top 11 for the next 12 years and in 1987 won more than £1 million, becoming the first British player to win the World Matchplay. Then, in 2001, he became the first player ever to win that tournament in three different decades and, at 43, the oldest ever winner.

Woosnam's game was blessed with all the ingredients of a winner – tenacity, bottle, passion, a powerful long game and a delicate short game. He has been a great golfer to watch.

He would surely have won more than one major – the 1991 Masters – had it not been for a slight weakness with the putter. While he didn't suffer quite as badly as Langer, it was miserable enough, but it never ate away at the rest of his game. He just kept peppering the pins.

And he hasn't done too badly: 44 tournament wins before he started playing on the European Seniors Tour. Woosie won in style, and he was a winning Ryder Cup captain too, in 2006.

◀ 'Tenacity, bottle, passion': Ian Woosnam dons the winner's green jacket after the final round of the 1991 Masters

infamous European Tour Qualifying School, graveyard of many aspiring golf pros, before he made enough cash on

The Greatest
Courses

St Andrews

The Scots invented golf, and this is where it all started. This is the home of golf.

There are more than 100 holes at St Andrews on the east coast of Scotland, but the main attraction is the Old Course. It's like nothing else on earth: pot bunkers, vast double greens, more bumps than a teenager's duvet and wonderfully springy turf.

You stand on the first tee staring at the widest fairway in the game and, minutes later, you're marching towards four hours of challenging, joyous golf.

And the best is saved for last … and second last: the 17th, arguably the most famous hole in the world, known as the 'Road Hole'. Making a double-bogey will never have seemed such fun. At the 18th, savour golf's most famous view as you aim your drive at the clock on the R&A clubhouse – and try to avoid hitting the old grey town on your right-hand side.

Think about who's played St Andrews – Bobby Jones, Jack Nicklaus, Arnold Palmer, Seve Ballesteros, Nick Faldo and Tiger Woods. And given the choice of only one golf course to play for the rest of their lives, some of these illustrious names would choose this above any other.

Augusta National

In the 1930s, a glint came into the eye of Bobby Jones, who had decided that winning golf tournaments had become a bit tedious. What better challenge than building one of the most beautiful golf courses in the world?

Jones teamed up with golf course architect Alister Mackenzie,

and together they created Augusta
National. And soon after the project
was completed, Jones instigated an
invitational tournament: the Masters.

by bunkers side and back, with Rae's Creek protecting the front.

To walk those carpet-like fairways and take in the fresh Georgia air, perfumed with the aroma of azaleas … could golf get any better?

Pebble Beach

Perched on California's rugged Monterey Peninsula, Pebble Beach is a spectacular spot – a gentle lob-wedge from the Pacific Ocean.

And the course has played host to some of the greatest US Opens: Jack Nicklaus in 1972, Tom Watson in 1982, Tiger Woods and his 15-shot win in 2000. But anyone can play at Pebble Beach. Just as at St Andrews, you can walk this hallowed turf.

The course's par-three seventh is small but scary. Its yardage barely makes it into three figures, but the line of play takes the golfer straight towards the Pacific, and it can get breezy. Bunkers and deep rough either side of the very narrow green aren't friendly. Even the pros get twitchy on this hole.

At the par-five 18th, the first two shots flirt with the ocean front, as the

The 11th, 12th and 13th at Augusta – the infamous loop of holes known as Amen Corner – are the most famous three holes in golf. They are also among the hardest.

The 11th features an unremarkable drive followed by an unnerving second, downhill to a kidney-shaped green guarded by water. The par-three 12th, played over water to a green a dozen or so paces deep, is the closest a pro gets to 'hit, hope and pray'. On the par-five 13th, after a 300-yard hook shot round the corner of the dogleg fairway, you're looking at a long-iron, off a sloping lie, to a green guarded fairway gently doglegs to the left. There was a time when the 550-odd yardage kept the green out of reach in two, but nowadays pros wing it on to the green with a drive and long iron. In the real world, though, it's still a fearsome finishing hole.

But don't think Pebble Beach is a two-hole wonder: it more than lives up to the hype.

Cypress Point

Next door to Pebble Beach lies Cypress Point – and it's no poor relation. In the golf magazine rankings, Pebble wins pretty much every time, but Cypress Point has its own charms and it's hard not to fall for them.

For starters, you've got the same gorgeous location. You've also got

▼ The crash of Pacific surf: the spectacular setting of Pebble Beach

THE GREATEST COURSES

▼ Cypress Point: gorgeous location, fantastic golf course

a fantastic golf course, designed by Dr Alister Mackenzie. The fairways meander through avenues of huge Monterey cypress trees, leading to heavily contoured greens where sculpted bunkers lie in wait.

If you're a big hitter, the front nine could be your happy hunting ground because it contains four par-fives and a couple of cracking par-threes. It's not monstrously long, either.

On the back nine there's no let-up in the entertainment stakes, for the emphasis is on shot-making. The par-three 16th is well over 200 yards, all of which requires an airborne carriage over the Pacific Ocean. It's a similar scenario on the intimidating but spectacular 17th. Slice your drive and you'll miss not just the fairway, but terra firma altogether.

No one ever came away from Cypress Point anything other than invigorated by one of the most enthralling experiences the world of golf has to offer.

Royal County Down

When Tom Watson first played this course, he said it included the finest consecutive 11 holes of links golf in the world. The other seven aren't shabby, either.

Book yourself a flight to Northern Ireland and a tee time, preferably when the yellow gorse is in bloom. You'll probably want to walk straight from the 18th green on to the first tee to do it all again.

If you don't fall in love with the front nine at Royal County Down, you surely aren't a golfer. In the mighty shadow of the purple and blue mountains of Mourne, the course follows the rugged curve of Dundrum Bay. You'll be captivated by the challenge that unfolds in front of you, described by Herbert Warren Wind as the sternest of any he'd experienced. But you'll get a stiff neck from looking over your shoulder at the stunning views.

Happily, the short fourth hole turns you to face the mountains for the first time. From there on there's no respite for the golfing senses, as verdant green fairways weave through golden swathes of gorse either side.

It can be uncompromisingly difficult, but this is one kind of punishment you could never get enough of.

▼ Verdant green fairways, golden swathes of gorse: the Royal County Down Club

Royal Melbourne

There are plenty of places with greater concentrations of golf courses than Melbourne. But few cities can boast such a cluster of top-quality layouts – and the best among them is the 36 holes to be found at Royal Melbourne.

The landscape is not dissimilar to that of a Scottish links, rugged and with an abundance of heather and bracken, and Scotsman Dr Alister Mackenzie had a hand in its creation, along with Australian Open champion Alex Russell.

Their success can be judged by the fact that it is the best golf course in Australia and one of the best in the world. Ernie Els says it's one of his favourite courses, and he believes Royal Melbourne has the best greens in the world.

But there are other reasons to make a pilgrimage to Australia: it's a classic all-round test of golf. The rugged bunkers represent avoid-at-all-costs hazards. The undulations of the fairways and greens take advantage of the rolling landscape, and it's a real shot-maker's course. The 18th is a simply magnificent par-four.

Royal Melbourne has a reputation as

▲ All-round test of golf: the 395m, par four 18th hole on the East Course at Royal Melbourne

▶ Jaw-dropper of a location: the 174 yard, par three 11th, 'Maidens', on the Ailsa Course at Turnberry a stern test of a golfer, but that doesn't detract from the pleasure it gives players of all standards. This is world-class golf for the masses.

Turnberry

The Ailsa Course nearly became a casualty of World War II. The old course, dug up to build an RAF airfield, nearly remained buried under concrete after the war. But it was rescued by architect Mackenzie Ross, and it was worth saving.

It has a jaw-dropper of a location on the west coast of Scotland, offering views across the Mull of Kintyre to the Isle of Arran. To the south-west, only Ailsa Craig, a giant Christmas pudding-shaped rock, interrupts the view.

But it took a single weekend of golf to put Turnberry truly on the map. In the 1977 Open, Tom Watson and Jack Nicklaus were locked in perhaps the greatest championship of all time. By the weekend, they had left the field trailing; they then battled head-to-head with shots of inspiration and brilliance. Only a single shot separated them at the end.

At Turnberry, you don't necessarily have to be a long driver, but you do have to be straight. This keeps you shy of wiry grasses and dunes, and enables

▼ Pine Valley: not your typical golf course

you to fire iron shots from the crisp turf and seek out the flags, usually tucked behind bunkers. It is an awe-inspiring test of golf.

Pine Valley

Businessman George Crump, a mad-keen golfer, had been looking for years for the perfect plot of land on which to build a course. Then he spotted Pine Valley – 200 acres of New Jersey forest and marshland – while looking out of a train window.

This isn't your typical golf course. The fairways are laid out like green carpets between vast expanses of trees, undergrowth, water and sandy scrubland.

Nowhere could the consequences of missing a fairway be more apparent. You know that if you hit it solidly off the tee, you may stand a chance of playing to your handicap. If you miss too many fairways, it's goodnight.

The greens are designed and protected in similar fashion, with cunning run–offs punishing slightly stray approach shots. Anything a little more wayward finds serious trouble. One of the greenside bunkers is called 'The Devil's Arse', which says it all.

Pine Valley members offer a standing bet to all first-time visitors, challenging them to break 80. Those members are a pretty shrewd bunch.

Valderrama

When billionaire Jaime Ortez Patino decided he wanted to build the Augusta National of Europe, he got in touch with golf course architect Robert Trent Jones and together they transformed an unremarkable layout in the south of Spain into continental Europe's finest course.

Valderrama is a fine championship test from the back tees and a very playable course from the more forward tees, so golfers of all standards can appreciate its charms.

The greens' grass is so fine that the putting surfaces are billiard-table smooth. The attention to detail is quite staggering and it makes the whole playing experience easy on the eye.

And technically speaking, it's a fine layout. There is a selection of holes that dogleg both ways, but the fairways aren't so narrow as to make the course unplayable to the average golfer. Instead, the main challenge lies in the second shots.

Cork trees tiptoe on to the fairway and partially block the line to the flag. Greenside bunkering represents an aesthetically pleasing form of added protection.

Whatever the numbers at the bottom of the scorecard, a round at Valderrama is something to savour.

Muirfield

An accurate barometer of a golf course's credentials is its roll call of championship winners. So let's dwell on the names of the golfers who have won an Open Championship at

Muirfield. Introducing Walter Hagen, Henry Cotton, Gary Player, Jack Nicklaus, Lee Trevino, Tom Watson and Nick Faldo … what more do you need to know?

Muirfield is one of the world's purest, fairest, stiffest, classic tests of links golf. Old Tom Morris, who originally penned the layout, and Harry Colt, who tweaked it into its current form, produced a masterpiece.

What you see is what you get. When you stand on the tee, everything is there in front of you: the ideal line, the hazards, all the information you need to pick the right shot. When you're staring at the green, it's the same story.

But Muirfield is a shot-maker's heaven on earth. The humps, hollows and undulations of the fairways and greens are made for golf. The 160 or so bunkers is an unusually high number, but at least you can see where they are.

Good shots get rewarded and bad shots get punished, although the capriciousness of the bounce can produce good or bad breaks. But if you're playing at Muirfield, it's your lucky day.

◀ The 18th green at Muirfield: what you see is what you get

21st Century Golf

A hundred years doesn't seem that long, but when you see that the game of golf in this period is bookended by the contrasting images of Harry Vardon and Tiger Woods, it suddenly seems an awfully long time. It barely seems the same game.

What would Vardon, James Braid and JH Taylor, who dominated golf around the start of the 20th century, make of the game today? We could put them on, say, Augusta National, persuade Tiger to make up a fourball and have him tee off first, so he could launch one of his drives 350 yards.

We'd kit out the old timers in long trousers – none of those silly plus-fours – and a soft cotton shirt instead of a starchy collar and tie. We'd swap their hickory-shafts for graphite, their crude clubheads for high-tech perimeter-weighted models with super grippy grooves, their woodenheaded drivers for titanium, and their primitive balls for high-spinning, long-distance, rubber bullets.

By then they'd scarcely recognise the game, although they might enjoy the extra 100-yard walk from the tee to their ball. Mind you, they're not used to 7,000-yard golf courses. It was more like 6,000 in their day. Still, we could arrange for an electric trolley… no, you can never beat a good old-fashioned caddie.

But is golf going to change as much in the next 100 years as it has in the last 100? Perhaps the more pressing question is: do we want it to change as much?

Golf's doing fine at the moment. We are in the era of the Tiger, who may be – barring interruptions such as we saw in 2010 as the fall-out from marital infidelities made world headlines – on his way to becoming the greatest player ever. But before Tiger came along, South African Ernie Els was touted as the man most likely to dominate.

Ernie won a hat-trick of South African titles – the Masters, PGA and

Open – in one season, an achievement that prompted Gary Player to say, "When I first saw Ernie play golf I knew I was witnessing one of golf's next generation of superstars."

Soon after joining the European Tour, he travelled to Dubai for the Desert Classic and tore the Emirates course apart, shooting a first round 61, 11-under par, that is regarded as one of the tour's greatest rounds.

Ernie then embarked on a global smash and grab of golf's trophy cabinet. In 1994, he won his first US Open at Oakmont, with a display of powerful hitting and assured holing-out. That year he won three separate world titles.

In 1997 he won his second US Open at the uncompromising Congressional Country Club. When the moment of truth arrived, on the par-four 17th, he struck a nerveless 5-iron that homed in on a pin placed perilously close to water: probably the shot of the year.

Els endured a few near misses between those two US Open wins, but he was gathering trophies fast and it was no big surprise when he triumphed in the 2002 Open Championship in a playoff.

◀ 'On a global smash and grab of golf's trophy cabinet': Ernie Els during practice for the 2006 HSBC World Matchplay at Wentworth

21ST CENTURY GOLF

▼ 'Effortless power and precision': Ernie Els raises his arms after winning the 1997 US Open

That week at Muirfield, all the best things about Ernie's game were in evidence. His second round 66 was a display of effortless power and precision. His final round stumble on the par-three 16th revealed a fallible side, but he shrugged it off by birdying the next hole and emerging triumphant from the playoff.

Later that year, Els played one of the most astonishing rounds in the history of the World Matchplay Championship, a 12-under-par 60 that lit up Wentworth's West Course. He then propelled his huge frame to new heights.

At the start of 2003 he averaged 65 over the four rounds of the Mercedes Championship, smashing the US Tour scoring record with his 31-under par aggregate. By the end of the year, he'd won seven times and bagged the top spot on Europe's Order of Merit. In 2004 he played surely the round of the year: a 12-under-par 60 at Royal Melbourne, a score that many thought impossible.

As defending champion of the Dubai Desert Classic in 2006, Ernie came up against a certain T Woods Esq in a one-hole playoff … and lost.

That Tiger should become the best player on the planet was no surprise; everyone saw him coming. His dad said Tiger had switched to an interlocking grip when he was still in nappies. He won three straight US Junior Amateur Championships, then three straight US shots); the largest winning margin (12 shots); the most shots under par for the back nine (-16); the most threes in one week (26) ... oh, and he was the youngest ever winner (21 years, three months and 14 days).

More remarkable even than that performance, Tiger won the centenary US Open at Pebble Beach in 2000 by 15 shots. In a week where no other golfer managed to finish under par, he

◀ Ernie Els with the Claret Jug after winning the 131st Open at Muirfield, 2002

▼ Tiger Woods with the trophy after his two-stroke victory at the Deutsche Bank Championship, 2006

Amateur Championships. Not even Bobby Jones could hold a candle to that kind of record.

In his first major championship as a professional, the 1997 US Masters, records fell like ninepins. Having played the front nine in a disappointing 40, he blitzed the back nine in 30 to finish with a two-under-par 70, then shot 66, 65 on Friday and Saturday. On Sunday, he cruised to a closing 69.

By the end of the week, Tiger was wearing a green jacket and he'd beaten Jack Nicklaus' lowest ever 72-hole total (270); set the largest 54-hole lead (nine was 12-under. That same year he won the Open Championship at St Andrews by eight shots, becoming only the fifth man to win all four of golf's major championships.

But even that Open win paled into insignificance when soon afterwards Tiger was in possession of all four major trophies at the same time. Technically, it wasn't a Grand Slam: it wasn't in the same calendar year. But in every other respect it was a Grand Slam, and it was nothing short of spectacular.

In 2003 and 2004, Tiger at least proved he's human. He continued to win tournaments on the PGA Tour, but he didn't win majors. By 2005, however, the Tiger was roaring again, racking up wins in the Masters and the Open Championship, and the following year saw him collecting his third Open victory and dominating the field to take the USPGA again.

Tiger's eyes, and those of the entire golf world, are on Jack Nicklaus' record of 18 professional major victories. For him to surpass that landmark is the loftiest of tall orders, but at the time of writing he can boast 14 major wins, the last of which came in 2008 when he walked away with the US Open trophy for the third time. In so doing, he equalled Nicklaus' record of winning each major at least three times.

Can anyone stop Tiger in his tracks? No. But check his stride from time to time and win more than just the occasional major? Phil Mickelson and Pádraig Harrington are just two of the possibilities.

Harrington, who attended the same Dublin school as fellow Ryder Cup player Paul McGinley – it must be something in the Liffey water – was nevertheless a late starter in professional golf. Unsure about his ability to make an impact and concentrating on his accountancy studies, he made his European Tour debut in 1996, when he was 25.

Since then, the victories, both in Europe and the US, have piled up to the extent that Harrington has 25 professional wins in his locker, and they include two of the biggies.

In a remarkable purple patch in 2007 and 2008, Harrington clinched back-to-back victories in the Open Championship and grabbed the 2008 USPGA crown with a two-stroke win. That made him the first European to win the USPGA in 78 years.

He's not the only current golfer from

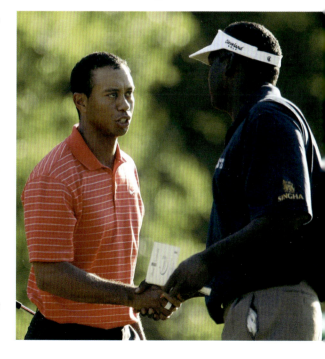

▼ Tiger Woods (left) shakes hands with Vijay Singh

21ST CENTURY GOLF

the island of Ireland to be making waves
– Graham McDowell and Rory McIlroy
are others – but Harrington has the
game and experience to go further.

Left-hander Phil Mickelson became
a major winner by taking the 2004
Masters in spectacular fashion, in

the most exciting Masters since Jack
Nicklaus took the title in 1986.

Phil put up an incredible back-
nine performance on that memorable
Sunday, pipping Ernie Els with a
last-hole birdie three. It gave him the
confidence he needed to challenge
anew for golf's top honours, and he
duly won the Masters again in 2006,
a year after he'd come away from
Baltusrol with the USPGA title.

Mickelson now has four major
titles in his locker, having finished the
2010 Masters with a 67 to beat Lee
Westwood by three shots.

There are many others aiming to
make their names in the glamorous

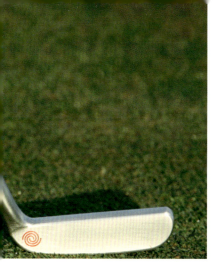

Mis-hits are no longer punished in the same way as 30 or 40 years ago. A 'necky' strike with a persimmon driver would see the ball take off low and slice weakly to the right. The same strike with an enormous titanium-headed driver produces a shot that is almost indistinguishable from a pure hit.

Golf ball technology has accelerated even faster. In real terms, the ball is responsible for probably an

◀ Modern technology: Phil Mickelson's putter and golf balls ...

▼ ... and irons and drivers

world of top-level pro golf, so we can safely say the game is in good hands. But is the equipment in the hands of the top players damaging the game?

Recent years have seen rapid developments in the way clubs are built, the materials used and the way they perform. The rules of golf control the dimensions and make-up of clubs, and the Royal and Ancient and the United States Golf Association watch developments keenly to ensure innovations conform. But shafts have got longer and lighter, clubheads have grown bigger and the properties of the materials used mean the ball comes off the clubface hotter and faster.

▲ Golf clubs: are their designs making great courses too short?

bunkers are being made redundant as pros drive straight over them.

It's becoming normal for par-fives to be reduced to a driver and mid-iron approach shot. Par-fours are frequently overpowered with a driver, sand-wedge approach, and often a driver isn't needed: a long-iron tee shot and mid-iron second are enough. As a result, classic layouts such as Sunningdale Old Course are considered too easy and too short to host a pro tournament.

Increasing yardages are now golf courses' main form of defence. The 2006 Masters, for example, was played over 7,445 yards, having been extended from 7,290 yards with the lengthening of six of Augusta National's holes.

The race to produce innovative equipment is continuing, even though the R&A and the USGA test it to ensure it conforms to the rules. Recent years have seen moves to limit the 'spring-like' effect of clubs and the updating of distance standards for balls.

But perhaps golf course design now needs to turn in two directions to satisfy the needs of both the amateur and professional game. You won't get too many average players queuing up to

extra 30 or 40 yards in the average drive of the leading tour pros over the last couple of decades.

It is argued by some that technology is in danger of ruining the game, and it has massive implications for the way golf courses are designed, for fairway play 8,000-yard courses.

While golf club technology has been going crazy, however, club golfers' average handicap has remained static. The equipment gets better, but we don't. To the average golfer, the improvement in equipment manifests itself in harmless, albeit pleasing, results.

Golf balls are more durable so don't need replacing as often – but they're just as easy to lose as they always were. Tour pros might be spinning balls back on the greens as if tugged on a piece of string, but the typical amateur is happy for the ball simply to stop somewhere on the green. Modern drivers make the ball go a bit further, especially on mis-hits, but certainly nowhere near as dramatically as in the pro game. Generally speaking, the benefits to amateurs are psychological.

So maybe we have nothing to worry about. Concerns over equipment technology are probably only relevant to the top 0.1 per cent of the golfing population. Joe Soap is not going to stop playing classic golf courses because they're no longer much of a challenge.

For the 99.9 per cent of people who play golf for fun, the game doesn't look set to change nearly as much in the next century as it did in the last. Even if the equipment looks different, the essence of the game will remain the same. It will always be engaging, entertaining, uplifting, challenging and at times infuriating. None of us would have it any other way.

▼ The game remains the same: the 17th hole (foreground) with the 18th and clubhouse behind on the Old Course at Sunningdale

Ryder Cup
Dream Teams

**The European Dream Team,
selected by Bernard Gallacher, 1995
Ryder Cup-winning captain**

Nick Faldo

Nick Faldo could genuinely intimidate
opponents. Just the appearance of his
name on a leaderboard was enough to
make people jump, and then there was
the sheer physical, 6ft 4in and 15-stone
presence of the man.

And Faldo played more Ryder Cup
matches, and won more points, than
any other golfer. In moments of intense
pressure, he came up with the goods.

In the 1995 Ryder Cup at Oak Hill,
playing the 18th against Curtis Strange,
Faldo was 100 yards from the pin and
needing to get down in two to win the
Ryder Cup. And he did exactly that,
pitching to four feet and holing the putt.

Under pressure, he was the man,
and Faldo's game was relentless in its
brilliance.

Seve Ballesteros

That Seve should strike what Jack
Nicklaus called "one of the greatest shots
I've ever seen," sums up his influence on
the Ryder Cup. Seve helped transform
the encounters from one-sided thrashings
into well-matched contests.

The shot Nicklaus was talking about,
against Tom Kite in 1983 at Palm
Beach, was a 3-wood from a fairway
bunker on to the final green. It only got
him half a point, but it was half a point
more than anyone else would have got.

Seve was the most exciting,
charismatic golfer ever to grace the
Ryder Cup, and his brilliance rubbed
off on others. When Jose Maria

Olazabal first played in 1987, the pair of them began the greatest partnership in the history of the competition.

Brian Barnes

Brian Barnes was a natural golfing talent who may not have fulfilled his potential. But he won his share of tournaments (10) and is known as the man who beat Jack Nicklaus twice in one day.

▼ Natural golfer: Brian Barnes lines up a putt

It was at Laurel Valley in 1975, when there were two singles matches in a day. In the morning, Barnes went out and thrashed the best player in the world 4&2. At lunchtime, Nicklaus said, "he's beaten me once, but he won't beat me again". But Barnes went out and gave him another hiding, this time by 2&1.

Great Britain & Ireland lost that Ryder Cup quite heavily. On the plane home, though, perhaps Barnes afforded himself a little smile of satisfaction.

Neil Coles

On paper, Neil Coles' Ryder Cup record might not look sensational, but his time coincided with a period of US domination.

Between 1961 and 1977, when Coles was a member of the GB&I team, the US won seven encounters and lost none. But in that time he compiled a highly respectable record, playing in 40 matches and being unbeaten in 19 of them.

Coles was a class act. His swing had a metronomic rhythm, whichever club he had in his hands. He caressed the golf ball with sweet timing and good technique and was one of the great fairway wood players.

If it hadn't been for a terrible fear of flying, Coles would have been far more famous, successful and wealthy than he became.

Tony Jacklin

Think of Tony Jacklin and the Ryder Cup and two images spring to mind: Jack Nicklaus conceding him a 30in putt at Birkdale in 1969 that meant the cup

For a while the best golfer in the world, he was the linchpin of the GB&I team for seven consecutive cups and in 35 matches he was unbeaten 21 times.

Jacklin as a player was awesome, as a captain even more so. That will probably be his enduring legacy.

Colin Montgomerie

Monty's Ryder Cup debut was a baptism of fire. At Kiawah Island in 1991 – the notorious 'War on the Shore' – he was thrust into the foursomes, alongside mild-mannered

◀ Class act: Neil Coles sinks a putt

▼ Victorious skipper: European team captain Tony Jacklin poses with the trophy after the 1985 Ryder Cup at the Belfry

was tied, and a smiling Captain Fantastic, leading Europe to victories at the Belfry in 1985 and Muirfield Village in 1987.

Jacklin deserves all the credit he gets for helping transform Europe into a team of world-beaters. It's a shame his playing performances aren't given more credence.

David Gilford, against one of America's 'tough nut' pairings – Lanny Wadkins and Hale Irwin.

They went down 4&2, but Monty was able to steady himself and come back to win a fourball, and then gain a fighting half against Mark Calcavecchia. Although the Cup was lost, Monty could hold his head high.

At the Belfry in 1993, he played like the European No 1 he was about to become. The Ryder Cup seems to bring out the best in Monty, as in the 2002 contest, when he led the victorious Europeans from the front, and in 2010 when he captained the winning team.

Sergio Garcia

The Spaniard could scarcely have made a more sensational Ryder Cup debut. Wearing European colours for the first time at Brookline in 1999, Garcia was in the morning foursomes on the first day, partnered with Jesper Parnevik against none other than Tiger Woods and Tom Lehman. Garcia and the Swede were magnificent, winning 2&1.

The pair went out in the afternoon and beat Phil Mickelson and Jim Furyk, then beat Payne Stewart and Justin Leonard the following morning. Three games, three wins.

Garcia lives and breathes the Ryder Cup, so motivation is not a problem for him. And he's a great matchplayer, as we saw at the 2002, 2004 and 2006 Ryder Cups when he formed a magical partnership with Lee Westwood.

Bernhard Langer

The German was the perfect playing partner – solid, dependable, making very few unforced errors and always holding his nerve. Add the fact that Langer captained the Europeans to a record

victory in 2004 – 18.5 points to 9.5 –
and you have a Ryder Cup legend.

Langer chose a tough year for his
first Ryder Cup, for at Walton Heath
in 1981 the US assembled its greatest
ever team. But around that time the
Europeans got the hang of winning,
and Langer played a critical role.

In the seven Ryder Cups after his
debut, he won many more matches
than he lost. It would have been fitting
had he holed that infamous putt on
the final green against Hale Irwin at
Kiawah Island.

Jose Maria Olazabal

With Seve Ballesteros, Ollie formed the
most successful partnership in Ryder
Cup history. Thrust into battle with his
inspirational countryman at Muirfield
Village in 1987, he thrived on the
pressure, at times appearing the stronger
of the two.

His sensational performance
helped Europe to their first victory
on US soil and Ollie's jig of delight
on the 18th green is one of the Cup's

▲ Ryder Cup
legend: Bernhard
Langer poses
with the trophy

▲ Thrives on pressure: Jose Maria Olazabal sprays champagne after victory over the USA in the 1997 Ryder Cup

▶ Peter Oosterhuis: better than 50 per cent record in the Ryder Cup

enduring images.

He was possibly on his way to compiling one of the Cup's most impressive records, but a foot injury sidelined him for two years. When he returned for the 1997 matches in Valderrama, he played a pivotal part in Europe's win.

This time Seve was his captain, not his playing partner. But the dynamic duo had struck again.

Peter Oosterhuis

Until Monty won seven straight Order of Merit titles, Peter Oosterhuis held one of the most impressive records in European golf, and between 1971 and 1974 he was Europe's numero uno.

Oosty was a fine player from a young age and was a seasoned campaigner by

the time he partnered Nick Faldo on his debut in 1977. The pairing won both their matches on day one.

Oosty won his last pro tournament at just 33, the same year he played in his swansong Ryder Cup. By then he had a better-than-50 per cent record from 28 matches, a fine effort during a lean period for the GB&I team. It's a shame he wasn't able to be a part of the European glory years.

Christy O'Connor Snr

The Irishman is a colourful character, but not even his personality could outshine his golf skills. One of Christy's favourite tricks was to stand on the tee of a medium-length par-

LITTLE BOOK OF **GOLF**

Talent like his doesn't go away overnight and even in the late 1990s, he was beating his age in professional senior championships.

Ian Woosnam

When Ian Woosnam played in his first Ryder Cup match, the 1983 encounter at PGA National, he told partner Sam Torrance on the first tee that he felt so nervous he was going to be sick. But Woosie came out fighting and started his round birdie, par, birdie.

That was typical of the man – a class player, a fine competitor, a man with serious bottle.

Woosie played in the next seven Ryder Cups and was one of Europe's true stars. He was involved in 31 games, won 14 and halved five – and

three and hit a ball on to the green with every club in his bag.

But it wasn't until he was in his mid-20s that he started to make an impact. In 1955, when he was about to hit 30, he first stepped into the breach on Ryder Cup duty. He was still playing when the cup went to Muirfield in 1973, when he was just coming up to his 50th birthday.

◀ Colourful character: Christy O'Connor Snr competes in the 1965 Ryder Cup at Royal Birkdale

▼ Fine competitor: Ian Woosnam poses with the Ryder Cup

RYDER CUP DREAM TEAMS

▶ Arnold Palmer: impressive Ryder Cup record

take into account the fact that in eight attempts Woosie never won a singles match. He makes it into the European dream team because of his exploits in fourballs and foursomes.

The United States Dream Team, selected by George Peper

Arnold Palmer

Who else could lead the US dream team? No other American has won more matches, and no one did it quite like Arnie. His golf game was an unparalleled cocktail of skill, brute force and bravado.

Built like a middleweight boxer, Arnie was not a fan of subtlety. His crushing drives and mighty iron shots were allied to one of the best chip-and-putt short games ever seen, and when he was on his game opponents were knocked over like ninepins.

His Ryder Cup record of 22 wins in 32 matches is justifiably impressive. As Lee Trevino once said, Palmer could attract a bigger gallery to watch him tie his shoelaces than most other golfers could muster with their best efforts on the course.

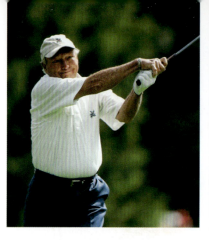

Jack Nicklaus

The way he dominated the tournament scene, you'd think Jack Nicklaus would have been invincible in a head-to-head confrontation. No one knew better how to bully an opponent psychologically than he.

But Jack suffered, if you can call it that, in his Ryder Cup career. Anyone who makes a Cup team can play a bit, and they might not have beaten Jack over four rounds. But in one round, anything can happen, and on eight occasions the Golden Bear got whupped.

But Jack travelled well and he wasn't fussy about which format he chose to win at. He played 28 matches and won 17, with another three halved.

Casper is best known for nailing Arnold Palmer in the 1966 US Open. Eight shots behind Arnie with only the back nine to play in the final round, Casper reeled him in like a giant fish on the end of a line, and the two were tied at the end. Arnie was the weaker of the two for the experience and lost the playoff.

Casper went on to win a US Masters – in a playoff. Evidently, head-to-head was his forte.

◀ Jack Nicklaus: won 17 of 28 Ryder Cup matches

▼ Billy Casper: head-to-head golf was evidently his forte

For anyone else, that would be a great record. Because it's Jack, we're surprised it's not better.

Billy Casper

Few golfers can claim to have played in eight consecutive Ryder Cups. That Billy Casper managed this, compiling an impressive playing record, explains what kind of golfer he was. He teed it up in 37 matches and in 27 of those he was unbeaten.

Lee Trevino: fierce competitor, but always had a smile and a one-liner ready

▶ Sam Snead: golf's most enduring talent and a Ryder Cup stalwart

Lee Trevino

For years, Lee Trevino worked at a driving range, collecting balls for a meagre income which he supplemented by playing money matches against all-comers. He famously said that real pressure was playing for 20 bucks when you only had 10 in your back pocket.

So Trevino was a rather useful matchplayer. Those money matches taught him all he needed to know about finishing an opponent off – but always with a smile and a one-liner. Trevino's six Ryder Cup appearances involved 30 matches and in 23 of those he was not beaten: one of the best Cup records.

He was one of the most gifted ball-strikers of his generation and, considering who was around at the time, that is saying something.

Sam Snead

Many say Sam Snead was the greatest natural talent who ever played golf. Certainly his was the most enduring talent of all. At a time when most people are looking forward to collecting their bus pass, Snead was still competing with the world's best golfers.

In matchplay, Slammin' Sam was awesome. His effortless long driving and classy iron play overwhelmed opponents and golf courses. It's just as well for the rest of the world's golfers that his putting wasn't red hot.

Not surprisingly, in the Ryder Cup he was pretty impressive. He played 13 matches and lost only two. Imagine what the GB&I players were thinking when they stood on the first tee and saw Snead. You'd hazard a guess they weren't overly optimistic.

the final green, which finished stone dead, was one of the greatest shots in Ryder Cup history.

He was unbeaten in 22 of his 33 matches. The 11 who took Wadkins' scalp can claim to have beaten one of the toughest matchplayers ever.

◄ Lanny Wadkins holds the Ryder Cup trophy

▼ Julius Boros drives off from the first at Royal Birkdale during the US team's 1965 win

Julius Boros

Julius Boros had a swing that was smoother than honey. It didn't just look the part, though; it also got the job done.

Not only was his game good enough to secure three major championships in an era that featured the likes of Jack Nicklaus and Arnold Palmer at the height of their powers, but to this day he remains the oldest person to have won a major. He clinched the 1968 USPGA Championship at the age of 48 years and four-and-a-bit months.

His game lost none of its potency in matchplay. In four Ryder Cups, Julius played 16 matches and lost only three. And keep in mind he was the grand old age of 47 when he played in his last Ryder Cup.

Lanny Wadkins

For the best part of two decades, Lanny Wadkins was a stalwart of the US Ryder Cup team. With his heart on one sleeve and the Stars and Stripes on the other, he played as though his life depended on it.

That he had bottle was never more evident than during the final-day singles at the 1983 Ryder Cup in Palm Beach. The US team was staring at home defeat, for the first time, when up stepped Wadkins. His wedge shot into

Larry Nelson

Serving in the Vietnam War probably put things in perspective. Larry Nelson did his time in that horrific conflict and after that, maybe a game of golf didn't seem so important.

Perhaps that's why he seemed impervious to pressure. Even in the biggest tournaments, he was able to keep playing his quietly efficient, methodical game.

Nelson's purple patch lasted less than a decade, but in that time he won a couple of USPGA Championships and a US Open. He also made an impression on the Ryder Cup: played 13, won nine and halved one.

Nelson didn't so much overpower a golf course as chip away at its defences. Opponents felt themselves subjected to similar treatment and, all too often, the experience proved painful.

▲ Larry Nelson: seemingly impervious to pressure

▲▲ Walter Hagen: almost unbeatable in head-to-head competition

Walter Hagen

Golf's ultimate showman wasn't averse to a bit of gamesmanship, like walking on to the first tee and saying: "Who's going to finish second, then?"

But Hagen had the 'go' to go with the 'show'. In fact, the man was virtually unbeatable in head-to-head competition. In the 1920s, when the USPGA was a matchplay event, he won it four times in a row, five times in all.

In his day, there weren't as many matches in the Ryder Cup as there are now, so in the five times he played he only had nine games. He won seven of them, though, and halved another.

Hagen was great in the true sense. Whether he was winning (frequently) or losing (rarely), his attitude did not change one iota.

Hale Irwin

He looked like a bank clerk, but he got his hands on a lot more money. Before he ditched his glasses and started dominating the US Seniors Tour, Hale Irwin was one of the fiercest matchplay competitors you could ever run into.

His game wasn't flashy, he didn't have

a flamboyant swing, nor did he hit the ball out of sight. But he drove the ball uncannily straight, kept his rhythm, hit a lot of greens in regulation, putted nicely and was able to stay calm under pressure.

Irwin compiled an impressive Ryder Cup record between 1975 and 1981. He then came back to Kiawah Island at the age of 46, won two matches and gained the vital half-point on the last green against Bernhard Langer.

Tom Kite

Winning majors might have been a problem for Tom Kite, but winning at matchplay definitely was not. The man was a ruthless slayer of European golfers.

In 1989 at the Belfry, he inflicted on Howard Clarke one of the heaviest defeats in Ryder Cup history – 8&7 – and in 1993 he annihilated Bernhard Langer by 5&3.

Not a long hitter, Kite used tee shots to get the ball somewhere near his 'patch' – inside 100 yards. With a wedge in his hands he was deadly, and he could putt a bit, too.

The worst thing for the Europeans who went up against him was that the

◀ 'Ruthless slayer of European golfers': Tom Kite

▼ Tiger Woods: will he become the greatest Ryder Cup points scorer of all time?

mental frailties that seemed to blight him in the major championships didn't seem to be a factor in matchplay.

Tiger Woods

Tiger's first few Ryder Cups were unspectacular affairs, during which he lost more than he won. But he was just getting into his stride.

If ever he stood a chance of getting turned over, this is the format to do it. Ryder Cup matches are only 18 holes, like a mad sprint for the finishing line. Anything can happen.

But Tiger will probably be playing Ryder Cup golf until at least 2016, by which time he'll have played in 10 of these things. Would you seriously bet that he won't be the leading points scorer of all time?

Who would win? The US dream team gets the nod by virtue of superior firepower. But we reckon it would be close. Call the scoreline 15-13.

Other books also available:

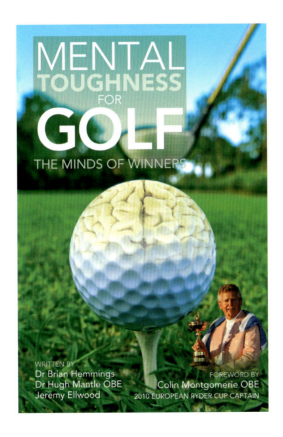

**The pictures in this book were provided
courtesy of the following:**

GETTY IMAGES
101 Bayham Street, London NW1 0AG

MEDIA WALES
www.mediawalesphotos.newsprints.co.uk

Design and artwork by David Wildish

Published by G2 Entertainment Limited

Publishers Jules Gammond and Alan Jones

Written by Patrick Morgan and Steve Newell